CONTENTS

FOREWORD   02
Tim Bullamore

INTRODUCTION   04
Maggie Lane

THE FINAL YEAR   10
Deirdre Le Faye

THE SUN OF MY LIFE   22
Amy Patterson

LETTERS: THEIR LEGACY AND LURE   32
Ruth Williamson

PEWTER AND PRAISE   42
Margaret C. Sullivan

JANE AUSTEN'S LITERARY LEGACY   52
Emily Brand

HER LEGACY TO NOVELISTS   60
Carrie Bebris

CLOSER TO JANE   68
Kim Wilson

PILGRIMS' PROGRESS   78
Susannah Fullerton

IMAGES OF JANE   88
Deirdre Le Faye

CAPTURING LIFE, NOT DEATH   102
Nigel Starck

LUST AND ATTRACTION   112
Penelope Friday

CONCLUSION: THE JOY OF JANE   122
Richard Jenkyns

FOREWORD

By Tim Bullamore

The concluding storms of a great conflict had hardly died down, when her world, almost unaware, bade farewell to Jane Austen; now, amid the closing cataclysms of a conflict yet more gigantic, we celebrate the hundredth year of her immortality. Time is the woodsman who fells the smaller trees and coppice in the forest of literature, and allows us at last to see the true proportions of its enduring giants; and the century that has passed since Jane Austen's death now sees her pre-eminence securely established.

Reginald Farrer – traveller, plant collector, eccentric and literary scholar – wrote those prescient words a century ago at the height of the First World War. While conflict raged in Europe, the literary world commemorated the 100th anniversary of Jane Austen's death, which itself had come soon after the end of the Napoleonic wars. Yet to read Austen's work is to find an oasis: not of calm, but of delight amid the anguish that seems so often to surround us.

As Farrer reminds us: "Wars may be raging to their end as the background of *Persuasion*, or social miseries strike a new facet of *Emma*; otherwise all the vast anguish of her time is non-existent to Jane Austen, when once she has got pen in hand, to make us a new kingdom of refuge from the toils and frets of life. Her kingdoms are hermetically sealed, in fact, and here lies the strength of their impregnable immortality; it is not without hope or comfort for us nowadays, to remember that *Mansfield Park* appeared the year before Waterloo, and *Emma* the year after."

Since Farrer's assessment – which appeared in *The Quarterly Review* and runs to almost 12,000 words – a great many others have had their say, and not only in the printed word. The intervening century has additionally given us films, stage shows and the internet to bring us closer to the world of which Jane Austen wrote so eloquently. The postal service that developed during Jane Austen's lifetime had changed little by the time Farrer composed his essay; yet a further 100 years later we can communicate instantly with almost anyone in the world via email and various brands of social media.

It had been our original intent, nonetheless, to reprint within these pages Farrer's essay in its entirety. However, such has been the wealth of offerings submitted by our correspondents that we can do little more than quote the handful of extracts that appear on this page. And to those correspondents I offer most profound thanks. This book makes no attempt to be a definitive summation of Jane Austen's life and achievements. It is, as the sub-title suggests, merely a selection of thoughts on the first 200 years of Austen's legacy.

Yet they are the most stimulating and diverse set of thoughts that any editor could hope to work with. I thank all our contributors: Deirdre Le Faye (twice); Amy Paterson; Ruth Williamson; Margaret C. Sullivan; Emily Brand; Carrie Bebris; Kim Wilson; Susannah Fullerton; Penelope Friday; and Nigel Starck. Particular thanks also to Maggie Lane for her erudite introduction and to Richard Jenkyns for his magisterial conclusion that so fittingly rounds off this volume.

Farrer, who died in 1920, not long after his authoritative essay appeared, concluded his work by showing why Jane Austen remains so celebrated:

A great friend of mine, a man who never opens a book by any chance, if a newspaper be to hand, finding himself shut up for weeks in a tiny Chinese town on the borders of Tibet, was driven at last, in sheer desperation of dullness, to Jane Austen. I watched the experiment with awe and anguish. I might have spared myself. Emma *baffled him indeed, but* Pride and Prejudice *took him by storm. And then, to my terror, he took up* Persuasion; *for surely of all her works, the appeal of* Persuasion *is the most delicate and elusive. But again I might have spared my fears.* Persuasion *had the greatest success of all; for days, if not weeks, my friend went mouthing its phrases, and chewing the cud of its felicities ... And when I tried to find out what had so specially delighted him in* Persuasion, *he suddenly and finally summed up the whole of Jane Austen and her work: "Why, all those people, they're – they're real!"*

TIM BULLAMORE is publisher and editor of *Jane Austen's Regency World* magazine

INTRODUCTION

As Jane Austen fans around the world commemorate the 200th anniversary of the author's death on July 18, 1817, aged only 41, **MAGGIE LANE** introduces *The Joy of Jane*, a tribute to the most loved writer in the English language

"What a pity such a gifted creature died so early!" Sir Walter Scott's lament, confided to his diary as he re-read Jane Austen's novels a few years after her death, has found echoes down the centuries and across the globe. But while sharing his regret, we might with equal justice give thanks that she was granted her 41 years of life; that she did *not* die of the fever caught at school in Southampton, as she might easily have done; that she grew up to write the six novels which have enriched, and continue to enrich, innumerable lives.

As recent scholarship has demonstrated, the circumstances of her life were by no means as wholly benign as her first biographers implied. But the proportion of anxiety and constraint she suffered to that of the familial support and intellectual stimulation she enjoyed was – another matter for thanks – exactly conducive to the creation of enduring art: art that has its depths and shadows as well as its joyous surface sparkle. Yet her background goes only so far in accounting for her achievement. The fact that her sister Cassandra, living under the same conditions and with the same genetic inheritance, did not write works of genius – or any works at all – confounds our feeble attempts to explain the mysterious alchemy that is literary creation.

We laugh out loud when we read Jane Austen, even across the gulf of 200 years of social change and even though we have encountered the jokes, the comic characters and the irony before – perhaps many times before. Her expressions are as familiar to re-readers (and who that loves Jane Austen does not repeatedly re-read?) as the most beloved lines of poetry committed to memory. In some respects she is the least poetic of prose writers – very few metaphors and very little description – yet in this respect, her ability to write memorable, perfectly honed and balanced sentences is truly poetic. Like poetry, her words bring solace and delight to our own journeys through life. Even as I write the words "very few metaphors" there comes into my head Mrs Elton's "very few lace veils". Mary Crawford says of Edmund Bertram, "he gets into my head more than is good for me". Jane Austen gets into our heads to our very great benefit indeed.

As this book explores, her legacy takes many forms. One of the conundrums of her art is its ability to sustain ongoing serious academic study in universities on every continent as well as the most trivial of marketing mania – and all points in between. These include societies, conferences, film, television, websites, tourism sites, museums, merchandise, magazines and books, books, books. Absurdly, perhaps, the number of words in print or online inspired by her exceeds by many multiples the words she wrote herself.

No other writer of any era or nationality pulls off quite this trick. Shakespeare perhaps comes closest in retaining his hold over our imaginations, and insinuating his language into our collective consciousness, but the Shakespeare "industry" is not so diffused – perhaps I should say, not so feminised. Where once Jane Austen belonged to the male academy, she is now the property of all

> One of the conundrums of her art is its ability to sustain ongoing academic study

kinds of groups and individuals with their different agendas.

It can be argued that all forms of pleasure we derive from the products of Austen's imagination are in their different ways legitimate, and fundamentally life-enhancing. Some admirers may choose to beaver away in archives, some learn dance steps, some visit places with a real or filmic connection and some seize on her characters to write their own novels or blogs. Some, of course, "just" like to read. Or listen. The pleasure of hearing her words spoken by a good actor (of either sex) for many people surpasses even their own silent reading. Which would Fanny Price prefer? We know that her pleasure in good reading was extreme. Appreciation of Austen's work can be a solitary enjoyment, undertaken in our own version of the East Room; or it can be the portal to a lifetime of good fellowship and shared pleasures. In celebrating the novels of Jane Austen, in whichever ways we personally find rewarding, we enlarge our knowledge of how life was lived in the past. We may even get a little closer to understanding the creative process.

What would Austen think if she could see what she has spawned? What would she think of the part of England in which she had her modest home (I was almost tempted to write, humble abode) signposted as Jane Austen country? What would she think of her name being all over the city of Bath, on buses and tea-rooms, that city which she was so happy to escape? And what would she think of the sight of several hundred people converging on her brother Edward's grounds every year to listen to some learned interpretation of her work, and

to picnic on the lawn (managing not to be rude to anybody). The cars in which they arrive would surely make her envy their drivers' – especially female drivers' – independence of movement; and when she heard that some visitors had actually *flown* across the Atlantic, or even from the other hemisphere, just to be in her village.... As for seeing the creatures of her brain take visual shape on a television screen – well, she would surely be divided between criticism when it was not done well and amazement that it could be done at all.

Response to the work of Jane Austen has shifted during the course of 200 years as some of the essays in this book explain. She has been appreciated variously as Dear Aunt Jane, as England's Jane, as one of the five pillars of the male-constructed Great Tradition, as the foremost female writer in an age of feminist literary criticism, as the first novelist whose every surviving word – letters as well as juvenilia and mature fiction – has been subjected to scholarly editing and publication. Her work soothed serving soldiers during the First World War and distracted at least two British prime ministers, Winston Churchill and Harold Macmillan, in times of stress. Beatrix Potter, whose fiancé had just died, took comfort as

IMAGE Beatrix Potter took comfort from the writing of Jane Austen

she walked the streets of Bath from considering how Anne Elliot was given a second chance of love; and for Alfred Tennyson the prime attraction of Lyme Regis was to see the steps where Louisa Musgrove fell. As for the eccentric Reginald Farrer, whose centenary essay set Austen criticism in a new direction, he considered that when mountaineering only two commodities were truly necessary in one's luggage, washing things and a set of Jane Austen's novels; and if one of those had to be dispensed with, it would be the washing things. Farrer it was who dubbed *Emma* "the book of books".

IMAGES Winston Churchill and Harold Macmillan were both distracted by Austen's work in times of stress

In our own times Jane Austen has, it seems, effortlessly surmounted the biggest hurdle to continued relevance, the great change in sexual mores of the past few decades. We certainly no longer care if a modern-day Lydia Bennet lives with a man before marriage. But we do still care that *Pride and Prejudice's* Lydia Bennet brings this shame on her family. We care, perhaps, because Elizabeth Bennet cares, and we love Elizabeth; but also because

Jane Austen's skill is to make her society and its value-system real and important to us. Her values, founded on the Christianity she was taught, are still fundamentally those of any civilised community, one that cares for its individuals, whatever religion or none we subscribe to, however modern we think we are. She does not need to preach, she dramatises moral choices and their effects on individuals, family dynamics, relationships and society. Indeed, if a religion consists of a set of moral values shared by like-minded adherents and supported by a sacred text, then appreciation of Jane Austen comes pretty close to becoming a religion in itself for a secular age. She is, uniquely among novelists, inexhaustible, offering what we need when we need it. As Ben Jonson said of Shakespeare, she is for all time. We do not know what the next 200 years will bring, but it seems safe to say that just as Shakespeare is still important to our culture 400 years after his death, so will Jane Austen be. We are lucky to have both.

MAGGIE LANE

Maggie Lane is Consultant Editor of *Jane Austen's Regency World* magazine and Editor of the Jane Austen Society of the UK's Newsletter

· · · · ·

THE FINAL YEAR

· · · · ·

Illness and worry plagued the last months of Jane Austen's life, and even taking the waters at Cheltenham could not restore her health, as **DEIRDRE LE FAYE** discovers

A s the year 1816 opened, Jane Austen could justifiably have felt that she had reached her pinnacle of success as a writer. She had published four unusual novels, the second of which had been a best-seller, and now her latest had been dedicated, by his request, to the Prince Regent. She was already halfway through a fifth text – working title *The Elliots* – and, after returning home from London in December 1815, she must have picked up her manuscript with renewed vigour to work towards reuniting Captain Wentworth and Anne Elliot.

But as her brother Henry remembered: "... the symptoms of a decay, deep and incurable, began to shew themselves in the commencement of 1816 ..." Her niece Caroline also recalled: "I beleive [*sic*] Aunt Jane's health began to fail some time before we knew she was really ill – but she became avowedly less equal to exercise." Jane had felt somewhat unwell before she left London and – again according to Caroline – had consulted the doctor who had attended Henry. Now, as winter turned into spring, she found herself growing inexplicably weak and suffering from recurrent bilious upsets, as she described them to herself. In 1964 the eminent physician Sir Zachary Cope was the first doctor to give close consideration to Jane Austen's terminal illness, as described by herself in her letters, and to form the diagnosis of Addison's disease, a diagnosis that has been confirmed by other doctors in recent years. In cold clinical terms, Addison's is a tubercular infection of the adrenal glands, which lie close to the kidneys and which are responsible for producing the necessary hormones cortisol and aldosterone. As the glands are destroyed slowly, the symptoms usually begin gradually and so are often ignored – they include increasing weakness with feelings of languor, gastrointestinal attacks, acute crises of fainting or faintness, bouts of fever and discolouration of the skin, especially in the face. There is no mental deterioration, and there are intermittent periods of improvement followed by decline. However, a stressful event such as a sudden illness or domestic calamity causes the patient to become acutely worse. This is called an Addisonian crisis and symptoms then can include sudden penetrating pain in the lower back, abdomen or legs, severe vomiting and diarrhoea, followed by dehydration, low blood pressure and loss of consciousness.

The onset of Jane's malady indeed probably dated back to the sudden shock and fright of Henry's near-fatal illness in October 1815. If she was already carrying some tubercular germ – and TB was rife at that period – this episode of great stress could well have caused the latent infection to activate and settle in the adrenal glands. From spring 1816 onwards Jane's own letters all too sadly confirm the progress of her disease and the family worries that hastened her end. To begin with, in February her brother Charles's command, HMS *Phoenix*, was shipwrecked off the Mediterranean coast near Smyrna. The ensuing court-martial accepted that the disaster had been the fault of the local pilot and Charles was fully acquitted of all blame, but for the foreseeable future he was back in London living with his in-laws on half-pay until another ship might be found for him – and in the postwar years this was likely to be a long wait.

The news of Charles's calamity abroad probably reached Chawton at much the same time as a second and even more distressing event occurred close at hand, on March 15 – the collapse of Henry's London banking business, Austen Maunde & Tilson, along with his country partnership of Austen Gray & Vincent in Alton. His governmental position as Receiver General of Taxes for Oxfordshire also disappeared in the bankruptcy proceedings. Nearly

IMAGE Henry Austen's country bank collapsed in March 1816

all the Austen family lost money, from Edward's £20,000 down to Jane's recent profits of £26.2s.0d. from her novels, and thereafter both Henry and Frank were unable to continue paying their annual £50 apiece towards the upkeep of their mother and sisters – such diminution of income being a permanent worry to the inhabitants of the Cottage.

Jane tried to keep cheerful, and it was probably during early May that she composed the spoof synopsis *Plan of a Novel*, when her niece Fanny Knight was staying at the Cottage

and could help to provide some of the jokes. But she evidently found herself now frequently unwell; and it may have been the Alton apothecary Mr Curtis who recommended her to visit Cheltenham and drink the spa water, as the town's advertisements claimed: "Almost incredible cures have been performed by it, when drunk on the spot." It was "singularly efficacious in all bilious complaints, obstructions of the liver and spleen, indigestion, loss of appetite ..." On May 22, therefore, Jane and Cassandra set off for Cheltenham, spending the first night of their journey

OLD WELLS & PUMP ROOM,
CHELTENHAM.

with James and Mary at Steventon. They stayed at Cheltenham for about two weeks and Jane drank the water of the Old Well: "The taste is slightly saline, and a small impression of bitter, like that of Epsom salt, is left upon the palate; but it is by no means so nauseous as most of the waters of the other wells," she noted. On their way back in early June they stayed for a few days with the Fowle family at Kintbury in Berkshire, and Caroline recalled: "Mary-Jane Fowle told me afterwards, that Aunt Jane went over the old places, and recalled old recollections associated with them, in a very particular manner – looked at them, my cousin thought, as if she never expected to see them again – the Kintbury family, during that visit, received an impression that her health was failing – altho' they did not know of any particular malady."

It would seem Jane had realised that the spa water had not helped her; but, despite her ill health, she continued to work on *The Elliots* and by July 18 thought she had finished it, with the re-engagement of Anne and Captain Wentworth effected in a scene laid at Admiral Croft's lodgings. Her nephew, James Edward, was staying at the Cottage for a few days and was able to give his first-hand account of

IMAGE Jane and Cassandra visited the spa in Cheltenham in May 1817

what followed. "But her performance did not satisfy her. She thought it tame and flat, and was desirous of producing something better. This weighed upon her mind, the more so probably on account of the weak state of her health; so that one night she retired to rest in very low spirits. But such depression was little in accordance with her nature, and was soon shaken off. The next morning she awoke to more cheerful views and brighter inspiration; the sense of power revived; and imagination resumed its course. She cancelled the condemned chapter, and wrote two others, entirely different, in its stead."

The ending of *Persuasion* as we now know it was completed on August 6 and as usual Jane put the manuscript aside until such time as she had satisfied herself, by many re-readings, that the text was ready for publication. She probably then returned to her old manuscript of *Susan*, which Henry had bought back earlier in the year from the neglectful publisher Crosby, and started to update it into the novel we now know as *Northanger Abbey*. This peaceful task received an unwelcome interruption later in the month when James's wife, Mary Lloyd, decided that she too wished to drink the Cheltenham spa water and required Cassandra to accompany her there. The thought of losing her sister's loving care, even if only for a few weeks, brought on the first of Jane's Addisonian crises, manifesting itself in pains in her back when Cassandra set off on August 28; and in early September Jane wrote to her: "Thank you, my Back has given me scarcely any pain for many days – I have an idea that agitation does it as much harm as fatigue, & that I was ill at the time of your going, from the very circumstance of your going –."

Cassandra returned to Chawton on September 21 and there is no further news of Jane's health until mid-December. Her niece Anna was now married to Ben Lefroy and living at Wyards, a farmhouse about a mile to the north of Chawton; and when Ben called at the Cottage on December 14 to invite Jane to dinner, she had to refuse, as she told James Edward: "... the walk is beyond my strength (though I am otherwise very well) ..."

The new year of 1817 opened more promisingly and Jane was strong enough to spend some days with her brother Frank and his boisterous children in their rented house in Alton. On January 23 she told Caroline: "I feel myself getting stronger than I was half a year ago, & can so perfectly well walk to Alton, or back again, without the slightest fatigue that I hope to be able to do both when Summer comes –." The following day she told her friend Alethea Bigg: "I have certainly gained strength through the Winter & am not far from being well, & I think I

understand my own case now so much better than I did, as to be able by care to keep off any serious return of illness. I am more & more convinced that Bile is at the bottom of all I have suffered, which makes it easy to know how to treat myself."

In this period of remission and hopefulness, on January 27 Jane started another novel – working title *The Brothers* – now known to us as *Sanditon*. She had planned it to be a long leisurely comedy with numerous characters in a cheerful seaside setting, and though she had been inconvenienced during February by what she thought was rheumatism, as she told Fanny Knight: "I am almost entirely cured of my rheumatism, just a little pain in my knee now & then, to make me remember what it was, & keep on flannel –." By March 1 she was working on chapter nine of the text. However, within a fortnight weakness overtook her again, and in her next letter to Fanny she could only say: "I am got tolerably well again, quite equal to walking about & enjoying the Air; & by sitting down & resting a good while between my Walks, I get exercise enough."

Almost immediately after sending this letter she had another crisis, and found herself too weak to sit up and continue writing *Sanditon*; the last date in the manuscript is March 18, and she left off half way through chapter twelve. This crisis was probably due to the knowledge that Mrs Austen's brother, Mr Leigh Perrot, now aged 82, was nearing his end. On March 24 Jane admitted to Fanny: "Indeed I shall be very glad when the Event at Scarlets is over, the expectation of it keeps us in a worry, your Grandmama especially ...." As for herself, she continued: "I certainly have not been well for many weeks, & about a week ago I was very poorly, I have had a good deal of fever at times & indifferent nights, but am considerably better now, & recovering my Looks a little, which have been bad enough, black & white & every wrong colour."

Mr Leigh Perrot died peacefully on March 28 and the next day Frank and Cassandra went to Scarlets to comfort their aunt. As her brother was childless and had always kept in close touch with Mrs Austen and her family, she was not unreasonable in expecting that he would remember them in his will. However, Mr Leigh Perrot's devotion to his wife was such that he left all his property to her for her lifetime, with the house Scarlets and a considerable sum of money being at her free disposal. After her death some of his money was to revert to James Austen and his heirs, plus £1,000 apiece to each of Mrs Austen's children who should survive Mrs Leigh Perrot – but all these legacies lay in the future, and so his death brought no improvement to the limited income of Mrs Austen and her daughters but a

huge disappointment to them instead.

On April 6 Jane told her brother Charles: "I have been suffering from a Bilious attack, attended with a good deal of fever. – A few days ago my complaint appeared removed, but I am ashamed to say that the shock of my

> The walk is beyond my strength (though I am otherwise very well)

Uncle's Will brought on a relapse, & I was so ill on Friday & thought myself so likely to be worse that I could not but press for Cassandra's returning with Frank after the Funeral last night, which she of course did, & either her return, or my having seen Mr Curtis, or my Disorder's chusing to go away, have made me better this morning." It was probably soon after this latest crisis that Anna and Caroline walked over from Wyards to call on her. "She was keeping her room but said she would see us, and we went up to her – she was in her dressing gown and was sitting quite like an invalid in an arm chair – but she got up, and kindly greeted us – and then pointing to seats which had been arranged for us by the fire, she said, 'There's a chair for the married lady, and a little stool for you, Caroline.' – It is strange, but those trifling words are the last of her's that I can remember ... I was struck by the alteration in herself – She was very pale – her voice was weak and low and there was about her, a general appearance of debility and suffering, but I have been told that she never had much actual pain – She was not equal to the exertion of talking to us, and our visit to the sick room was a very short one – Aunt Cassandra soon taking us

away – I do not suppose we stayed a quarter of an hour; and I never saw Aunt Jane again ..."

Over the next few days Mr Curtis, the Alton apothecary, admitted that he could help no further, so the family called in Mr Giles-King Lyford, a doctor at the Winchester Hospital, and his medication gave her some relief. Jane must by now have realised that it was unlikely she would recover, and so on April 27 privately made a short

unwitnessed Will, in which she left £50 to Henry and £50 to his old French housekeeper Mme Bigeon, who had lost her savings in Henry's bankruptcy, with Cassandra as residuary legatee.

Henry wrote later: "Her decline was at first deceitfully slow; and until the spring of this present year [1817], those who knew their happiness to be involved in her existence could not endure to despair. But in the month of May, 1817, it was found advisable that she should be removed to Winchester for the benefit of constant medical aid, which none even then dared to hope would be permanently beneficial." On May 22 Jane told her friend Anne Sharp: "An attack of my sad complaint seized me ... the most severe I ever had – & coming upon me after weeks of indisposition, it reduced me very low. ... My head was always clear, & I had scarcely any pain; my cheif [sic] sufferings were from feverish nights, weakness & Languor. – This Discharge was on me for above a week ..." Two days later James's carriage took Jane and Cassandra to Winchester, with Henry and her nephew William Knight riding beside as escorts.

The sisters' old friend Mrs

IMAGES Left, Jane Austen's unwitnessed will. Right, the parlour in College Street, Winchester, where she spent her last few weeks

Heathcote, who lived in the Cathedral Close, had taken lodgings for them at Mrs David's house, No 8 College Street, and it was here that Jane passed the last weeks of her life. She wrote to James Edward, now an Oxford undergraduate, assuring him that the lodgings were very comfortable and that she was continuing to get better – with ironic humour to the last: "Mr Lyford says he will cure me, & if he fails I shall draw up a Memorial & lay it before the Dean & Chapter, & have no doubt of redress from that Pious, Learned & disinterested Body." In this context, a memorial was a quasi-legal document, a petition or claim made to some person or body in authority; hence Jane is saying that if

Mr Lyford cannot cure her, she will sue him from beyond the grave and expects the Winchester clerics to adjudicate and award her damages. In fact, Mr Lyford had already told the family privately that her death was imminent.

Cassandra naturally was in constant attendance and Henry visited frequently, writing afterwards that: "She supported, during two months, all the varying pain, irksomeness, and tedium, attendant on decaying nature, with more than resignation, with a truly elastic cheerfulness. She retained her faculties,

IMAGES Below, Winchester Cathedral c1801. Right, Jane's family paid for her ledger stone

In Memory of
JANE AUSTEN,
youngest daughter of the late
Rev.d GEORGE AUSTEN,
formerly Rector of Steventon in this County
she departed this Life on the 18th of July 1817,
aged 41, after a long illness supported with
the patience and the hopes of a Christian.

The benevolence of her heart,
the sweetness of her temper, and
the extraordinary endowments of her mind
obtained the regard of all who knew her, and
the warmest love of her intimate connections.

Their grief is in proportion to their affection
they know their loss to be irreparable,
but in their deepest affliction they are consoled
by a firm though humble hope that her charity,
devotion, faith and purity, have rendered
her soul acceptable in the sight of her
REDEEMER.

her memory, her fancy, her temper, and her affections, warm, clear, and unimpaired, to the last." Mary Lloyd rode over from Steventon on several occasions to help her sisters-in-law; and when Jane had another crisis between June 9 and 13 and thought she was dying, she said then: "You have always been a kind sister to me, Mary." However, she recovered slightly and drifted on, ever downwards, until the middle of July. On St Swithin's Day, July 15, she dictated her last verses, "When Winchester races first took their beginning ...", joking about the saint's probable disapproval of the horse races that were advertised to take place outside the city later in the month. That evening she collapsed again and remained only partly conscious until her final collapse on the evening of July 17. Mary Lloyd wrote in her diary "Jane Austen was taken for death about ½ past 5 in the Evening" and on July 18: "Jane breathed her last ½ after four in the Morn: only Cass & I were with her Henry came."

Before the coffin was closed, Cassandra cut off several locks of Jane's hair for family keepsakes and wrote two long letters to Fanny Knight with minute details of Jane's last hours. Henry made all the arrangements for the funeral to take place in Winchester Cathedral on Thursday, July 24, with the grave being dug in the north aisle. The fact that Jane was buried inside the cathedral has been a puzzle for many

biographers, since she had no obvious connection with Winchester and at that date was not famous for her novels. The reason is simply a mercenary one: the Dean and Chapter had decided in November 1809 that burial within the Cathedral itself could be granted on a sliding scale of charges: 50 guineas for burial in the choir, 20 guineas for burial in the aisles and parts adjacent to the choir and above the steps, and ten guineas for burial in any other part of the church. In November 1816 they added that permission for burial should be conditional on a ledger stone of a uniform size being laid down, "ranged in order with such as already exist". As the family knew that Jane had greatly admired the cathedral, they were prepared to pay 20 guineas for a place in the north aisle; and a year later, in October 1818, to lay the engraved stone on the grave cost them a further ten guineas.

As she finished her first letter to Fanny, Cassandra wrote with sad resignation: "The ceremony must be over before ten o'clock as the Cathedral service begins at that hour, so that we shall be at home early in the day, for there will be nothing to keep us here afterwards." Fanny did not visit Chawton again until November, when she saw her grandmother and aunt still suffering the grief and emptiness of bereavement, and wrote in her diary:

"A melancholy meeting! And everything looking so sad!" Her final entry for the year 1817 was: "I had the misery of losing my dear aunt Jane Austen after a lingering illness."

DEIRDRE LE FAYE

Deirdre Le Faye has been researching and publishing accurate original information regarding Jane Austen's life since 1975. In 2014 the Royal Society of Literature awarded her its Benson Medal for her work in this respect

SOURCES

Henry Austen: 'Biographical Notice of the Author', prefixed to first edition of *Northanger Abbey* and *Persuasion* (1818); and reprinted in J.E. Austen-Leigh, *A Memoir of Jane Austen, and other family recollections*: ed Kathryn Sutherland (Oxford University Press, 2002).

Caroline Austen: *My Aunt Jane Austen*, a memoir (Jane Austen Society, Chawton,1952, 1991).

Reminiscences of Jane Austen's niece Caroline Austen: ed Deirdre Le Faye (Jane Austen Society, Chawton, 1986, 2004).

Fanny Knight's Diaries: ed Deirdre Le Faye (Jane Austen Society, Winchester, 2000)

Deirdre Le Faye: *Jane Austen, a Family Record* (Cambridge University Press, 2nd edn 2004).

Jane Austen's Letters: ed Deirdre Le Faye (Oxford University Press, 4th edn, 2011)

Sir Zachary Cope: 'Jane Austen's Last Illness' in *British Medical Journal* July 18, 1964, II, 140, 182-183; also Jane Austen Society, Collected Reports I (1949-65), 267-272.

A Guide to all the Watering and Sea-Bathing Places: ed John Feltham (London, n.d., post-1817).

Information from Dr Cheryl Kinney, Texas, 2016.

Information from Dr David Rymill, Cathedral Archivist, Winchester, 2015-16.

THE SUN OF MY LIFE

· · · · ·

AMY PATTERSON considers the role of sisterhood, both in the novels and in Jane Austen's life

My Dearest Fanny –
Doubly dear to me now for her dear sake whom we have lost.

Thus begins Cassandra Austen's letter to her niece Fanny announcing the death of Jane Austen in the early hours of July 18, 1817. It's a sentence that many Austen fans know by heart. After all, Jane wasn't the only Austen woman who could take your breath away with the first line. When I visited Jane Austen's House Museum in Chawton at Christmas 2009, I found this letter tucked quietly away outside what was once Martha Lloyd's bedroom, perched next to a window overlooking the well-kept gardens. It was the kind of thing that I may have passed by if I had not already known what those first three words, in that flowing, steady hand, signified.

I have lost a treasure, such a sister,
such a friend as never can have been surpassed. She was the sun of my life, the gilder of every pleasure, the soother of every sorrow; I had not a thought concealed from her, and it is as if I had lost a part of myself.

Cassandra's letter is a monument to joyful, exuberant love interrupted by the bitter cruelty of profound loss. Her friendship with Jane was not merely a typical sister relationship – not even for the time they lived in. They were forced to depend on each other in ways that went beyond any sister relationship Austen drew in her novels.

Although Jane was 41 when she died, she and her sister were only just starting the first chapter in what was meant to be their book of independent

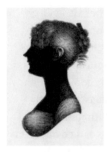 

IMAGES Cassandra Austen and Martha Lloyd

living. They had miraculously survived penury roulette, being shuffled from brother to cousin to friend and back again after their father's death in 1805. Another death – this of their brother Edward's wife after the birth of her eleventh child – brought a sudden reprieve when he offered the sisters and their mother a small cottage on his Hampshire estate at Chawton. They moved there in 1809 and, for the first time after years of upheaval, Jane Austen sat down to write, edit and publish four works within the first five years of living in Chawton.

The cottage, from a view two centuries later, looks like a second spring of youth for the sisters. They brought their friend Martha Lloyd to live with them; I'll refrain from imagining them staying up past midnight trying on clothes and having pillow fights. They were, after all, well past the years of flirting. But

definitely not past the years of gossip.

There is a heady, spinning, exhilarating sort of "early parts of *Romeo and Juliet*" feeling to all of it. You know, all the laughing and the strolling and the speaking in rhyming verse. Jane even included some of it in a letter to her brother Frank in a poem congratulating him on the birth of his son:

> *Our Chawton home, how much*
> *we find*
> *Already in it, to our mind;*
> *And how convinced, that when*
> *complete*
> *It will all other Houses beat*
> *That ever have been made or*
> *mended,*
> *With rooms concise, or rooms*
> *distended.*

Having said that, it's the early parts of *Romeo and Juliet* that always make my mother cry the hardest. Every time we see any version, whether it's on stage or the 1968 Zeffirelli film, or even the one with *Leo!*, she cries and says: "I can't handle it! They're just so happy, and you know they're going to die! Oh … kids, slow down!"

> *Her looks altered and she fell*
> *away, but I perceived no material*
> *diminution of strength, and, though*
> *I was then hopeless of a recovery, I*
> *had no suspicion how rapidly my*
> *loss was approaching.*

The time at Chawton just wasn't enough after all. In the end, all Cassandra could do was hold Jane in her arms and ease her struggle. They weren't even at home, but in Winchester for medical care when Jane died. The sisters are buried nearly 20 miles apart, for all eternity – Cassandra in sleepy Chawton and Jane at Winchester Cathedral, her tomb perpetually beneath the noisy feet of hundreds of thousands of tourists every year.

When Jane was born their father, the Rev George Austen, wrote in a letter: "We have now another girl, a present plaything for her sister Cassy, and a future companion. She is to be Jenny." Although the nickname didn't stick – and thank goodness for that, as I'm not sure how many copies of "Jenny Austen's *First Impressions*" would fly off the shelves – the companionship certainly did. The girls carved out their own dainty personal space from a house taken over by a school for boys, with a sitting room next to their shared bedroom. And we know from the surviving correspondence between Jane and Cassandra that they shared a bond that allowed them to express the kind of sly sarcasm we all share with our siblings or our best friends: "I give you joy of our new nephew, and hope if he ever comes to be hanged it will not be till we are

IMAGE Anna Maxwell Martin and Anne Hathaway played the sisters Cassandra and Jane in Becoming Jane (2007)

too old to care about it." (April 25, 1811)

This type of communication was a vital part of the sisterly bond for them, and Jane undoubtedly trusted her older sister in ways that she did not trust others. She certainly wrote things to Cassandra in her letters that she would never want anyone else to know she had written. Austen gets some criticism for this cattiness now but, to be fair, that is probably only because several of her letters have survived to be published, while the neighbour who called her a "husband hunting butterfly" doesn't have anyone coming around offering her great-great-grandchildren millions of pounds for a scrap of paper with a scribble of her writing on it. (Actually – I must correct myself – that particular neighbour was the mother of the noted author Mary Russell Mitford. Maybe her great-great-grandchildren would stand to get a few thousand. Start digging, kids!)

I would venture that things haven't changed much for sisters in the intervening centuries when it comes to communication, except perhaps the style and the technology. When I was young and adventurous, I decided I was going to be a scientist – a conviction that stuck for only slightly longer than Jane's decision to be Mrs Harris Bigg-Wither, and which burnt just as many bridges. While we can't ask Jane why she turned down the Bigg-Wither gig, I can tell you that I sympathise; a lack of organisational skills and a severe dearth of willingness to maintain a cleanroom environment would have done me in, both in the thin films lab and Georgian Hampshire. But my studies temporarily took me 2,000 miles from home, to the desert of New Mexico. And my sister simultaneously embarked on a study abroad journey to the English Midlands.

One thing older sisters never seem to believe is how truly dependent we younger ones are on their example to get our heads around how we're meant to live. Even though my mother had pretty accurately labelled us as "the Elinor" and "the Marianne", I think my sister still believed in her heart of hearts that it was all a bit of a joke. But Austen makes it painfully clear to Elinor, and to any big sister reading *Sense and Sensibility*, that we second daughters need all the guidance we can get. And so my sister and I, thousands of miles apart, talked more that year than we had in the five years before. Absence, heart, fonder: you know the deal. Picture Lydia, unwilling to write to her own mother but sending so many letters to Kitty "much too full of lines under the words to be made public" that Kitty is the only one unsurprised by the elopement with Wickham. *Not that I ever did anything that needed to be underlined, mom, I swear!*

But when I read accounts of

"young Jane Austen", with her brash verbal humour and her fearless family theatricals, I wonder if there is this

still and listen and be pretty and take lessons, and then rejoice in being young Miss Firstname, whose job it is to pull ribbons and pout and scream and be a Holy Terror in general. Second children, no matter how well-behaved, know from the moment they are born that they are in direct competition for their parents' attention. And Jane – "Jenny" – was merely the second *girl*. She was common thread that runs through all younger sisters. When I remember that she wrote fearless Lydia Bennet – and even the bold Elizabeth Bennet, let's be fair – I have to assume that Jane recognised a certain impertinence in younger sisters, a certain ability to look up at Miss Lastname, whose job it had been for all those years to be first, to sit the *seventh* child. I can only imagine what Cassandra must have put up with.

My sister certainly put up with a lot. She started piano at age five. I was three – I just *had* to tag along as well. And to art and dance too! This was, incidentally, right about the age at which my mother first read *Pride and Prejudice* to us, stopping to explain things like "entailment" and "elopement" and "if you keep hitting your sister you will have to sit in timeout".

Northanger Abbey, Sense and Sensibility and *Pride and Prejudice* were

IMAGES Above, the Bennet sisters in the BBC's 1995 *Pride and Prejudice.* Right, Hattie Morahan (Elinor) and Charity Wakefield (Marianne) in *Sense and Sensibility* (2008)

all initially composed during Austen's early years of writing, before the long years of silence that followed her father's death. Cassandra would have been nearby for the composition of the most interesting scenes, offering advice and encouragement. But it wasn't only through Cassandra's friendship that Jane would have absorbed the sister love that she poured into her books. Mrs Cassandra Austen's sister Jane Cooper was a dearly loved Aunt Jane in her own right, whose death as a result of the typhus outbreak that sent the girls home from their boarding school would foreshadow another Cassandra without her Jane decades later.

One of the most touching sister scenes in Austen's work is the sickbed scene in *Sense and Sensibility*, when Elinor sits helplessly as Marianne almost succumbs to an illness brought on by her misery over Willoughby's betrayal. "She was calm, except when she thought of her mother; but she was almost hopeless; and in this state she continued till noon, scarcely stirring from her sister's bed, her thoughts wandering from one image of grief, one suffering friend to another." From a young age, Jane would have had the example of her mother living

on without her only sister to inform Elinor's grief.

The idea of sister loss would come back much later in Austen's writing career. Two of the most annoying women in literary history, Miss Bates and Mrs Elton, are each half of a sister relationship that's no longer what it once was. Miss Bates's long chatty soliloquies are begging for the soothing interruption of the voice of a sister who understands. At the start of *Emma*, it's been 18 years since Henrietta Bates's younger sister Jane Fairfax (née Bates) died of "grief and consumption" and a dozen since her niece Jane, for several years "the property, the charge, the consolation, the foundling of her grandmother and aunt", was taken by Colonel Campbell as a companion for his daughter. This arrangement surely spared Miss Bates and her mother from poverty, but their loneliness must have been extreme.

Through all those long paragraphs of babble you can almost hear a silence, an opening where the voice of a more sensible sister would interrupt, or punctuate – agree, or caution, or silence too harsh a thought. Austen shows us a similar if much less likeable relationship in the Miss Steeles in *Sense and Sensibility*. The older spinster sister Anne lacks Miss Bates's simple friendly charm, but she shares a need for sororal intervention:

"Nay, my dear, I'm sure I don't pretend to say that there an't. I'm sure there's a vast many smart beaux in Exeter; but you know, how could I tell what smart beaux there might be about Norland; and I was only afraid the Miss Dashwoods might find it dull at Barton, if they had not so many as they used to have. But perhaps you young ladies may not care about the beaux, and had as lief be without them as with them. For my part, I think they are vastly agreeable, provided they dress smart and behave civil. But I can't bear to see them dirty and nasty. Now there's Mr Rose at Exeter, a prodigious smart young man, quite a beau, clerk to Mr. Simpson, you know, and yet if you do but meet him of a morning, he is not fit to be seen.– I suppose your brother was quite a beau, Miss Dashwood, before he married, as he was so rich?"

"Upon my word," replied Elinor, "I cannot tell you, for I do not perfectly comprehend the meaning of the word. But this I can say, that if he ever was a beau before he married, he is one still for there is not the smallest alteration in him."

"Oh! dear! one never thinks of married men's being beaux – they have something else to do."

*"Lord! Anne," cried her sister, "you
can talk of nothing but beaux; –
you will make Miss Dashwood
believe you think of nothing else."
And then to turn the discourse, she
began admiring the house and the
furniture.*

Young Jane Bates was also likely not as
cunning a little sister as Lucy Steele, but
she may have spared her older sister the
mortification of talking for too long on
subjects not meant for others to hear.

The Bateses home is already a
depressing picture of spinsterhood, but
when added to it is the thought that
each treasured letter from Jane Fairfax
carries with it the memories of letters
from another Jane Fairfax, long dead;
that Jane's grandmother, nearly deaf
and shortsighted, must be at pains to
trace the features of a beloved daughter
in the graceful face of the quiet young
woman she sees less and less frequently;
it becomes clearer why Miss Bates,
always a silly woman, has still never
lost the love and respect of the elders of
the neighbourhood. Even if she never
explicitly mentions the loss of her sister,
her every word and action broadcasts
that she lives in a state of upheaval that
the steady hand of a young woman
on whom she must have doted, as she
does Jane, could only have helped to
settle. Emma, perhaps, is too young to
realise how much of a void is left by

the sister who may have been the only
person to listen to her monologues with
patience, or respond to her voluminous
kindhearted gossip with equal
enthusiasm.

As unsympathetic as Mrs Elton
paints herself to be, she is another
woman in Emma's circle who is crying
into the void of sister loss. She and Miss
Bates seek out each other's company

> Children know from the
> moment they are born
> that they are in direct
> competition for their
> parents' attention

in an increasingly needy cycle of social
dependence. Her sister's Maple Grove
marriage has put her in a social circle
beyond what poor Augusta can hope
to achieve, and Selina doesn't seem to
be making much of an effort to include
the new mistress of the Hartfield
Vicarage, as the long hoped for visit in
Mr Suckling's *barouche-landau* never
materialises.

Toxic sisterhood is elsewhere in
Austen. The Elliot sisters in *Persuasion*,
while in parts cruel and demanding, are
angels compared with the sisters
in *Mansfield Park*, the ultimate literary
sister cat fight. Like other Austen works

the book is ostensibly about the marriage plot, but it truly follows the unravelling of Maria and Julia Bertram – a process that can be traced back to the totally psycho-sister dysfunction outlined in the first paragraph of the novel.

Aunt Norris, the most twisted sister in the history of the English novel, takes it upon herself to disrupt the relationship between Lady Bertram and Mrs Price, and also to poison any goodwill between the sisters Maria and Julia Bertram by encouraging the jealousy and competition that eventually leads to the dissolution of Maria's marriage to Mr Rushworth and her elopement with Henry Crawford.

These disastrous sisterhoods reoccur in Austen's literature, even appearing as early as the juvenilia, including *The Three Sisters* and *The Watsons,* which Austen abandoned as early as 1805. As far as Cassandra's remaining collection of letters demonstrate, we don't have evidence to show that these portrayals are autobiographical. Some fanciful fans would argue that perhaps it is the letters Cassandra destroyed which hid years of arguments and betrayals between her and Jane that would have inspired such caustic sister narratives.

Of course, I think that Jane Austen was simply a good author with a powerful imagination and the ability to create entire characters out of whole cloth. Not too hard to imagine for most of the world's best authors, but for some reason people seem to want to assign autobiography to Austen's works. Perhaps it's because she writes so conversationally that we feel as if we know her personally. Some readers want to believe that her world and her works were the same place and she walked between them seamlessly. Maybe they believe that if she did, they could too.

These creative world-walking powers were at their peak when she created the sisterly masterpiece of *Mansfield Park*. While we're probably supposed to be happy for Fanny Price winning the hand of Edmund, perhaps the least romantic suitor of all time, it isn't the triumph over his heart that truly shows Fanny's strength. In fact, at Portsmouth she has all but given him up, and it's only through her finally recognising her strength as a sister, instructor and role-model for young Susan Price that Fanny realises her worth.

Cassandra did famously burn much of her correspondence with Jane after her sister's death, thereby preserving Jane's character and her privacy from future generations of snooping fans and biographers. Over the years theories as to why she burnt the letters have ranged from the romantic – hiding evidence of Jane's secret string of love affairs – to the mundane – perhaps she simply didn't feel like keeping the dusty old things around anymore. But while it's the letters between the two of them that tell us the most about Jane Austen herself, it's in writing to Fanny Knight, the niece who Jane called "almost another sister", that we learn the most about what life would be like for Cassandra after Jane left her alone in Winchester on that July morning in 1817.

> *I watched the little mournful procession the length of the street; and when it turned from my sight, and I had lost her for ever, even then I was not overpowered, nor so much agitated as I am now in writing of it.*

Cassandra could not even attend the funeral with her brothers, because in those days it was improper for a woman to do so. She watched the procession as it went down the street and turned the corner, as she had watched over her little sister Jane so many times in their lives. She would have watched Jane playing in the dirt in their mother's kitchen garden, of which she was so proud. She would have watched a teenage Jane go out and tend to the brewing and wine-making. She would have watched Jane dance and flirt and make a spectacle of herself doing "everything most profligate and shocking in the way of dancing and sitting down" with young men. She was

always there, either as a companion or at the other end of a fond letter. These two sisters, tethered to each other for mutual comfort both financial and emotional, made their way in the world together for 41 years, until separated at last by Jane's final illness.

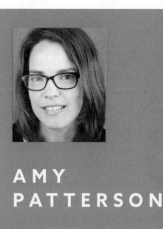

AMY PATTERSON

Amy Patterson is a freelance journalist living in northeast Ohio, where she and her monther and sister operate Jane Austen Books, the only book store in the world specialising in books by and about Jane Austen: **janeaustenbooks.net**

. . . . .

LETTERS: THEIR LEGACY AND LURE

· · · · ·

Jane Austen's surviving letters offer a fascinating insight into her life and thoughts. **RUTH WILLIAMSON** looks at how they were dispersed after her death and have since been collected by historians

On Sunday April 27, 1817, Jane Austen wrote her last will and testament. Apart from three small separate bequests, "every thing of which [she] might die possessed" was given and bequeathed to her sister, Cassandra Elizabeth Austen. The will also appointed Cassandra sole executrix. When Jane died less than three months later, on July 18, her only sister took custody of the manuscripts and letters left behind. That Cassandra saw her role, and the duty she felt she owed to her late sister, as a sacred trust seems certain. She took admirable care of Jane's literary bequests and, before her own death in 1845, she carefully allocated the unpublished fiction manuscripts to surviving brothers, nephews and nieces.

Jane Austen's personal correspondence received different treatment. According to family tradition Cassandra retained the letters that her sister had written to her for most of the long years that passed between 1817 and the end of her days. She burnt the majority of the correspondence and removed some content from the remaining letters two to three years before she died. In the view of Caroline Austen, the younger daughter of Jane's eldest brother James: "Aunt Cassandra would have been indignant had correspondence between [Jane and Cassandra] been read and commented upon [even] by their own nieces and nephews, little or great."

IMAGE A letter from Jane to Cassandra that dates from 1799

Cassandra controlled just what material was passed on to the next generation of the family. If Austen scholars and biographers are frustrated by this today, two hundred years later, some who actually knew her regretted as early as the 1860s that "materials ... have ... been buried out of our sight by the past generation". By 1913, James Austen's descendants were openly attributing to Jane's generation of Austens "a great hatred of publicity" and to Cassandra herself feelings "so precious ... [that it] would have seemed to her nothing short of profanation" had strangers dwelt upon the memory of her sister.

Yet Cassandra did preserve what she deemed to be appropriate for the next generation. By carefully apportioning what she allowed to remain to selected relations, she may have considered that the particular material she passed on to each was of most significance to that individual. The practical outcome of this division of mementoes, of manuscripts, and especially of letters, was that one branch of the family had little or no idea of what another might possess or know.

When Cassandra died in March 1845, readers might not yet be clamouring for more information about the late author of *Pride and Prejudice*, but some demand there was, and it grew. The fortunate owners of Jane's surviving letters were sitting upon a potential goldmine, or a powder keg, depending upon perceptions of the contents of her correspondence.

None of Jane's letters written to her brothers James, Edward (Austen Knight) or Henry had been retained. On the other hand, her brother Francis (Frank) kept her missives carefully. He also preserved those that she had written to his first wife, Mary.

Unfortunately, after he died in 1865 his youngest daughter Fanny-Sophia destroyed the latter resource without referring to anyone. Frank had not been immune to approaches from admirers of his sister's works. He sent one of Jane's autographs to a Miss Hutton in 1841 and one of her complete letters to the Quincy family in the United States in 1852. It appears that Jane's youngest

brother Charles kept only the very last letter he received from her. The division of her correspondence among branches of the Austen family posed significant challenges to those who aimed to accumulate her personal information as the years passed. Her favourite niece Fanny (Knight, later Lady Knatchbull) and James Austen's daughters Anna (Austen, later Lefroy) and Caroline (Austen) did keep the letters that they had received from Aunt Jane, but they were not of one mind regarding how much of that material might be made public.

Even so, a market was developing inexorably for "souvenirs" and later for substantial collections of Jane Austen's original correspondence. Fanny Knight's son, who published Jane's letters to his mother in the "Brabourne edition" in the 1880s, sold some of the originals thereafter. He charged £5 for the sale of one letter to a dealer in 1891, while apologising that "[m]ost of these letters are signed only 'JA' altho' they are undoubtedly genuine". In the early 20th century collections were acquired by J. Pierpont Morgan, Charles Hogan and Alberta Burke in the US, and back in the UK Lord Rosebery paid £1,000 for a single letter in 1933. By 1909, Jane's letter to Cassandra dated June 11, 1799, had reached the National Library of Australia in Canberra,

IMAGES Left, J. Pierpont Morgan collected Austen's letters in the early 20th century. Above, James Edward Austen-Leigh (c1864), who recognised the increased interest in her life

where it remains. Her autograph alone commands a hefty investment in the 21st century. In May 2005 the asking price for a fragment of a letter was US$7,500. Dispersal had gathered momentum after the passing of the generations who had known the author in person.

Her nephew, James Edward Austen-Leigh, did remember her and recognised the increased interest in her life by the 1860s. He approached members of the wider family, as well as his sisters Anna and Caroline, to prepare a more detailed biography than had been produced before. In it he included a note of apology for his aunt's letters, since she "would probably have been capable of looking more deeply into the heart of things, had any impulse from outside induced her to try".

Other branches of the family proved reluctant to release "relics" that they held. For instance, Austen-Leigh was not able to consult the letters from Jane to Fanny Knight. Then, in 1884, only two years after Fanny's death, her son, the first Lord Brabourne, published his late mother's collection of letters from Jane, including those that she had inherited written by Jane to Cassandra. Brabourne's edition, in two volumes, was not a full transcription of the letters. References he considered unsuitable for publication were omitted and, instead of satisfying the public's thirst for biographical information, the volumes led to further conjecture. Nor did the edition receive universal acclaim. In his introduction he referred to previously unpublished content – notably Jane's letters to her sister – and claimed that it "afford[ed] a picture of her such as no history written by another person could give". Furthermore, it was his view that "before one can thoroughly understand and feel at home with the people of whom Jane Austen writes ... one should know something of the history of Godmersham". His vaunting of material that had been unavailable to Austen-

Leigh, and a focus upon his own social milieu, did not go unnoticed. He was criticised for being ponderous and dull. A review by Mrs Humphry Ward even regretted the loss of literary reticence as a virtue.

Other editions followed. In 1908 one published in Newport, Rhode Island, included a preface by Sarah Chauncey Woolsey (whose pen name was Susan Coolidge), author of *What Katy Did*. In her opinion "the letters, in all probability, are carefully chosen to reveal only the more superficial side of their writer... [We are given] a glimpse of ... Miss Austen's life; and the glimpse is a sweet and friendly one. We are glad to have it, in spite of our suspicion that another and even more interesting part of her personality is withheld from us." Reservations about information withheld persisted.

Criticisms of the *Letters'* "limited" subject matter and "narrow" scope became all too familiar to Dr Robert Chapman, Austen's scholarly editor of the 20th century. He, like Brabourne, published a two-volume collection of the *Letters*. Its appearance in 1932 (for Oxford University Press) crowned 20 years of work. Some, like Mary M Lascelles, a long-term tutor at Somerville College, Oxford, who belonged to Chapman's network of academics, regarded his collection as the "climax, though not the conclusion of the Austenian studies". But once again the *Letters* had a mixed reception. Those passages suppressed previously were now revealed, because Chapman saw no reason to withhold them. Jane Austen had made unkind sport of conditions as unequal as bad breath and stillbirth in her private correspondence, and such comments resulted in a sharp readjustment of her reputation. Credit is due to Chapman for including this "unsanitised" material in the face of the criticism that followed.

"Her letters have had some detractors and some apologists," he noted, but he saw "no need for apology". Rather, he celebrated the "characters" in the correspondence

IMAGES Left, Mrs Humphy Ward, who considered the Brabourne edition of Austen's letters to be ponderous and dull. Above, Robert Chapman's collection, published in 1932, was regarded as the "climax, though not the conclusion of the Austenian studies"

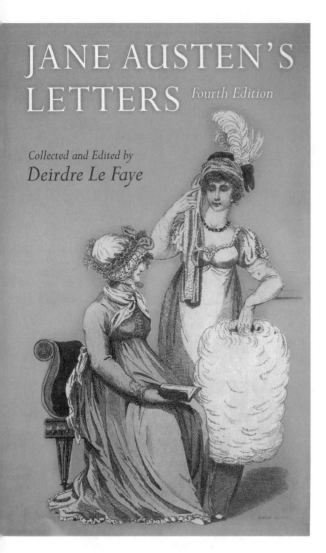

JANE AUSTEN'S
LETTERS *Fourth Edition*

Collected and Edited by
Deirdre Le Faye

writers and commentators such as E M Forster and Harold Nicolson, who rejected the *Letters'* content as trivial and, worse, dull. Forster wrote that Austen's letters were "catalogues of trivialities which do not come alive ... they have not the magic that outlasts ink". Nicolson concluded that "[s]he emerges diminished". Despite charges that Jane Austen the letter writer was unlikeable, Chapman remained her champion and rebutted such views by pointing out that "the novelist had a genius for the particular" and in her letters "the eager interest ... in matters of domestic concern ... is scarcely less infectious".

Chapman edited a second edition in 1952, but as more Austen family information was uncovered and other small portions of letters were

and found Austen's observations and criticisms to be "in the same class as the material of the novels".

Lascelles believed that he must have been hurt by the opinions of

discovered, the need for an updated edition arose. Deirdre Le Faye compiled it after years of painstaking research. Her third edition (for OUP) appeared in 1995 and a fourth was required by

2011 to incorporate continuing Austen scholarship, new details about her life and family and revised bibliographical material.

Some 200 years have now passed since Jane Austen's letters came from her pen. They record details of domestic life, but readers may also identify her personal tastes within them. It is clear that she knew what was expected of letter writing. When she wrote to Cassandra between January 3 and 5, 1801, she commented: "I have now attained the true art of letter-writing, which we are always told is to express on paper exactly what one would say to the same person by word of mouth. I have been talking to you almost as fast as I could the whole of this letter."

This is her playful interpretation of received wisdom, such as appeared in *The Complete Letter-Writer*: "When you sit down to write a letter, remember that this Sort of Writing should be like Conversation [and should] express Nature without Affectation."

According to advice quoted in *Converse of the Pen*, a letter should "wear an honest, cheerful countenance, like one who truly esteems and is glad to see his Friend; and not like a Fop admiring his own Dress and seemingly pleased with nothing but himself". While personal correspondence might provide the opportunity for some self-expression, in Austen's lifetime the writer often adopted a polite persona because letters were often read aloud in social circles and fully discussed. Readers of Jane Austen's letters may decide for themselves whether or not she always retained a disguise.

Her collected letters may have challenged some conventions, but there is no doubt that they have furnished historians of the period with an invaluable record of the domestic concerns of a single lady with limited means. Knowledge of her domestic minutiae has extended far beyond the correspondence.

These letters could not have been written by anyone other than the author of her novels. There are connections of vocabulary, phrasing and style between the letters and fiction that stamp both as hers. She has her creation Miss Bingley say that "a person who can write a long letter, with ease, cannot write ill". Austen herself acknowledged the challenge posed by sitting down to write a letter without having a great deal to say, although she practised the regimen of sustained application until the flow of ideas resumed to her satisfaction. That approach must also have supported her writing of fiction. She knew the reality of a writer's life. While she provided her niece Anna with nuggets of good advice about writing, she understood just as well the distractions posed by domestic duties.

Jane Austen was acutely aware of the fine margin between domestic comfort and genteel poverty. When her father was about to retire to Bath in 1801, Jane wrote that he was "doing all in his power to increase his income by raising his tithes etc" and, optimistically, she did "not despair of [his] getting very nearly 600 a year". For one whose means were modest in life, how ironic that her literary legacy continues to generate so much discussion and profit more than 200 years later.

Austen possessed "the miracle of communication" as Chapman termed it. Today, letter writing may be a dying art, given present-day technologies and lifestyles. Yet there are still some who try to emulate its former appearance: enthusiasts have devised a "Jane Austen font" so that electronic missives may be sent and received to look as if she has written them. Another enterprising devotee has set up a means of connecting pen friends through an Austen letter writing club online, while making it clear that matchmaking is not the object. Perhaps the epitome of such homage takes the form of personalised letters composed from the phrases Jane Austen wrote, and even "signed" by the lady herself.

The letters that she actually wrote continue to inspire contemporary fiction, and they represent an unparalleled resource for learning about the woman who left the world a legacy of six remarkable novels and other writings. It is in her letters that she came closest to personal disclosure. The possibility of future discoveries of her lost letters is remote, but even the slightest prospect of one more is irresistible.

IMAGE Lord Brabourne published the collection of letters from Jane to Fanny Knight, his late mother, in 1884

SOURCES

Caroline Austen, *My Aunt Jane Austen*, Jane Austen Society, 1952.

Jane Austen, *Jane Austen's Letters*, Third Edition, ed. D Le Faye, OUP, 1995.

W and R A Austen-Leigh, *Jane Austen's Life and Letters*, 1913.

W Austen-Leigh, R A Austen-Leigh & D Le Faye, *Jane Austen, A Family Record*, British Library, 1989.

B Brophy, "Jane Austen and the Stuarts" in *Critical Essays on Jane Austen*, ed. B Southam, Routledge, 1968.

R W Chapman, Introduction to the First Edition, Jane Austen's Letters (1932), reprinted in *Jane Austen's Letters*, Third edition, ed. D Le Faye, 1995.

E M Forster, *Abinger Harvest*, London, Edward Arnold 1936.

D Graves, "Vocabulary Profiles of Letters and Novels of Jane Austen and her Contemporaries", *Persuasions Online*, Vol 26, No 1.

C Harman, *Jane's Fame*, Text Publishing Co, 2009.

C Houlihan Flynn, "The Letters" in *The Cambridge Companion to Jane Austen*, eds, E Copeland & J McMaster CUP, 1997.

Mary M Lascelles, *Jane Austen and her Art*, OUP, 1939.

D Le Faye, 'Letters' in *Jane Austen in Context*, ed Janet Todd, CUP, 2005.

Cheryl L. Nixon and Louise Penner, "Writing by the Book" in *Persuasions Online*, Vol 26, no.1, 2005, quotes *The Complete Letter-Writer*.

Bruce Redford, *Converse of the Pen: Acts of Intimacy in the 18th century Familiar Letter*, University of Chicago Press, 1986.

R Sales, *Jane Austen and Representations of Regency England*, Routledge, 1996.

James & Horace Smith, *Rejected Addresses: or the New Theatrum Poetarum*, October 1812.

K Sutherland, *Jane Austen's Textual Lives from Aeschylus to Bollywood*, OUP, 2005.

C Tomalin, *Jane Austen, A Life*, Viking (Penguin Group), 1997.

Barbara Britton Wenner, "'Following the Trail of Jane Austen's Letters", in *Persuasions* No 27, 2005.

RUTH WILLIAMSON

Ruth Williamson is a writer, an active member of the Jane Austen Society of Australia, and contributes to the literary scene in Australia, Canada and the United Kingdom in addition to her native New Zealand

• • • • •

PEWTER AND PRAISE

· · · · ·

The Jane Austen 'industry' is a substantial economic force – and
it began with the author herself working professionally with her
publishers, as **MARGARET C. SULLIVAN** writes

Jane Austen fans love Jane Austen's work; that is a given. Those six novels, and the collected unfinished, unpublished, and shorter works, are the sacred text and the well of our affection. The novels are what we, as Janeites, all have in common. Thus it is not very surprising that some Austen fans were chagrined to discover that some authors have taken to writing sequels and prequels to Austen's novels, and remixing them as well – writing "variations", in which a crucial plot point is changed and the characters sent careering off on a whole new tangent unimagined by Austen herself, or rewrites of Austen's plots in a different time and place, with the familiar story changing in reaction to the setting. And then there's the zombies, the vampires,

the werewolves and other supernatural manifestations invading Austen's stories with their bloody fangs and yen for brains.

To say that some Janeites love these subsidiary works and some loathe them is rather too simplistic; there are as many different ways of loving Jane Austen as there are Jane Austen fans. There is the relatively self-contained group of enthusiasts for what they call JAFF, an acronym for Jane Austen Fan Fiction. JAFF started online, as stories published both on Austen fan sites and fan fiction archives that cater to writers from many fandoms. However, unlike most fandoms, Austen's work is in the public domain, and the authors can publish their fan fiction without "filing off the serial numbers", as fan writers for more recent fandoms have been forced to do if they wish to publish their work – to rewrite it without reference to the original, copyrighted work. (The *Fifty Shades of Grey* series, for example, was originally fan fiction written by a fan of Stephenie Meyers's *Twilight* series.) And publish it they have, the vast majority inspired by *Pride and Prejudice*, remixes of Elizabeth and Darcy's relationship or explorations of the inner lives of minor characters such as Georgiana Darcy or the younger Bennet sisters, often adding generous dollops of the drama and passion that modern readers crave. In recent

IMAGE Curtis Sittenfeld has written a modern version of *Pride and Prejudice*

years these books have been mostly self-published, and some may look down upon them for that fact alone. That attitude is unfair and unworthy of a Jane Austen fan.

But not all those publishing Austen-inspired books are enthusiasts or would consider themselves to be fan fiction writers. A recent series, written by well-regarded authors such as Joanna Trollope and Curtis Sittenfeld, takes Austen's novels and sets them in the 21st century. Respected genre authors such as P. D. James and Colleen McCullough both produced sequels to *Pride and Prejudice*. These books had the imprimatur of the commercial publishing industrial

complex, commanding a certain amount of grudging respect from even the most rabid anti-JAFFer, though they seem to appeal less to dedicated Janeites and more to the world at large.

Now Hollywood, and even the BBC, have turned from their periodic enthusiasm for filming Austen's novels and have started filming the fan fiction, such as James's *Death Comes to Pemberley*, while the bone-crunching tome of Austenian zombie mayhem, *Pride and Prejudice and Zombies*, had a big-screen release. Online web series such as the *Lizzy Bennet Diaries* are a fresh, modern take on Austen's stories that have been joyously embraced by Janeites of varying levels of canon purism.

If the media properties are not enough, then there's the merchandise – playing cards, tote bags, T-shirts, jewellery, knitting patterns inspired by Jane Austen's work, the famous action figure, and much, much more. Even the most tolerant Janeite, one who enjoys the remixes and the tchotchkes, has occasionally considered the question: what would Jane Austen have thought of it all?

While I have been one of those dastardly authors who have dared to play around in Jane Austen's world, and I own no fewer than three of the action figures, I would not presume to declare Austen's thoughts on the matter, as that seems like more of an affront than just sending her characters on new adventures. Such speculation would probably be an exercise in projection, anyway, as I tend to identify with Austen as a fellow writer as well as my favourite author. Many Janeites have studied Austen's biography, but it has always been the aspects of Austen as a professional author that have most fascinated me. And make no mistake: she was as professional and business like as any 21st-century entrepreneur author, despite her retired country life.

Austen became a professional author when she sold her first manuscript. That was *Lady Susan*, now known as *Northanger Abbey*, which she sold to B. Crosby and Company in 1803 for ten pounds. An inauspicious beginning, perhaps, but we all have to start somewhere. Crosby never published the novel and Austen eventually bought back the manuscript, but nonetheless someone paid her for her writing and therefore Jane Austen was a professional author. However, she wouldn't be a *published* author for another eight years.

Publishing in Austen's time was fraught for authors, and not necessarily well paid – in other words, rather like being an author today.

IMAGES Left, a scene from *Pride and Prejudice and Zombies*. Right, the famous Austen action figure

An author might sell her copyright outright to the publisher, which most authors preferred as the payment was guaranteed and all risk placed on the publisher if the book did not sell well. However, if the book was a bestseller, the author did not necessarily receive more money.

The most common method of publishing in Austen's time was on commission. The publisher would have the book composed and printed and the author would receive all profits less a 10 per cent commission to the publisher. However, the author would only see profits once the printing costs were recovered – and paper was very expensive, not to mention the cost of labour, delivery and advertising. This

yours affectionately
John Murray

Thomas Egerton under the commission system in 1811. Austen was realistic about her chances as a first-time author, and she fretted about possibly owing money to Egerton, setting aside as much as she could of the small allowance that she received from her brothers. This anxiety turned out to be misplaced, as the book sold well enough that Egerton offered to purchase the copyright of her next book, *Pride and Prejudice*, for £110. Austen felt that she deserved £150, but was pleased that she would receive a guaranteed payment.

Egerton published *Pride and Prejudice* frugally, using an inferior grade of paper, and charged readers more than he had for *Sense and Sensibility*. Knowing that *Pride and Prejudice* has always been Austen's most popular work by far, it is easy to guess what happened – Jane Austen wrote a popular, best-selling book, and her publisher received most of the profit. Get as indignant as you like over Austen seeing no profit from the zombie stuff; she did not even get her due in her own lifetime.

Austen never sold a copyright again. She published her next two books, *Mansfield Park* and *Emma*, on commission. Jan Fergus, the Austen scholar, has suggested that Austen delayed publishing *Persuasion* and *Northanger Abbey* not because she was ill at the end of her life, but because she

method placed the risk on the author; if the printing costs were not recouped, the author could actually owe the publisher money. Any publisher trying to get authors to cover their losses these days would have the wrath of the internet called down upon them, but even in these modern times plenty of authors receive a small advance for their book, and no more.

Austen's first published work, *Sense and Sensibility*, was published by

IMAGE John Murray: "he is a Rogue of course, but a civil one", wrote Austen

wanted to save money to defray any costs of publishing those two books. She was determined to publish. She loved to write. But like any professional, she loved to get money for her writing, too:

> "... tho' I like praise as well as anybody, I like what Edward calls Pewter too." – Letter to Fanny Knight, November 30, 1814

Austen carefully saw her books through the publication process. She proofread the pages as the printer produced them, met publishers, wrote letters and endorsed the cheques that she received in payment for her work. When Crosby failed to publish *Lady Susan*, Austen wrote to him under a pseudonym demanding that the book be published or the manuscript returned to her. She thought and acted for herself, as a professional should.

If you ever get a group of authors together, eventually they will start complaining about their publishers. Jane Austen was no different. She complained about the poor offers her publishers made for the copyrights of her novels, the slowness of the printers and the high prices the publishers charged for the books. Of John Murray, who published *Emma* and the second edition of *Mansfield Park*, she wrote, "... he is a Rogue of course, but a civil one."

Difficulties with publishers could not keep Austen from writing. While she suffered from the debilitating symptoms of her final illness, she worked on the book that would eventually be called *Sanditon*, though she did not live to finish it. Criticism did not keep her from writing, either. She collected what she called "opinions" of *Mansfield Park* and *Emma* from friends and relatives. Most of these opinions were critical but not too painful – the readers preferred *Pride and Prejudice* to *Mansfield Park* (some things never change) or liked Miss Bates and Mrs Elton but couldn't bear Emma Woodhouse – and some of them were positively gushy, but some of them ... well, one hopes that Jane recorded them because she found them hilarious, not in some bizarre spasm of self-abuse. They *are* hilarious, though her fellow writers will cringe a bit in sympathy. A Mrs Augusta Brownstone "owned that she thought S & S. – and P. & P. downright nonsense, but expected to like M.P. better, & having finished the 1st vol. – flattered herself she had got through the worst." Of *Emma*, a Mr Cockerelle "liked it so little, that Fanny wd not send me his opinion." One suspects that Mrs Brownstone and Mr Cockerelle would find themselves quite at home leaving book reviews on Amazon or Goodreads. Perhaps the opinions are the real reason that Austen, in the famous story from James Edward Austen-Leigh's *Memoir* of his aunt, asked that a squeaky door at Chawton not be repaired so that she could hear anyone approaching as she sat in the parlour writing. Perhaps it was not, as many scholars have opined, because she didn't want the neighbours to know that she was an author; perhaps it was so that she didn't have to discuss her work in progress with every morning caller with an opinion.

A professional author takes these things in her stride. She does not respond to the critics; if she chooses to read the reviews, she enjoys the kind and happy ones, learns from the

IMAGE Joanna Trollope rewrote Jane Austen's *Sense and Sensibility*

constructively critical ones and ignores, or better yet laughs at, the silly and ignorant and grumpy ones. Austen collected the opinions and I think – I hope – that she laughed at them. The author of those six novels, I think, would laugh.

Authors in the 21st century may think we have invented branding, but I think that Austen made an attempt to brand her first two novels. She published anonymously, so they could not be advertised as "Jane Austen novels". However, she retitled each book from its working title, giving them paired alliterative titles: *Elinor and Marianne* became *Sense and Sensibility*, and *First Impressions* became *Pride and Prejudice*. By the time *Mansfield Park* was published, the popularity of Austen's novels meant that she was no longer completely anonymous. She still did not put her name on her books, but even the Prince Regent knew who she was. Branding via title was no longer necessary, and it's become an accepted truth among Janeites that the title of Austen's third novel was a reference to the judge Lord Mansfield who oversaw court cases related to slavery, surely a title with more meaning to Austen within the context of the novel. (Maybe she could have titled it *Mansfield and Morality*.)

"...the truth is that the Secret has spread so far as to be scarcely the

Shadow of a secret now—& that I beleive whenever the 3d appears, I shall not even attempt to tell Lies about it. —I shall rather try to make all the Money than all the Mystery I can of it." – Letter to Francis Austen, September 25, 1813

It can be fun to speculate where Austen's career would have gone had she lived as long as her parents and most of her siblings. Another thirty years of Jane Austen novels would be something. I think *Sanditon* would have been the breakout novel, the one that

PARLOUR IN CHAWTON COTTAGE, WITH JANE AUSTEN'S DESK

firmly established the Jane Austen brand as such. If everyone had to know who Jane Austen was, she would make all the money she could out of it, as any professional would do.

By the time *Emma* was published Austen had three successful books in that brand. The subjects of her novels had already evolved as she gained financial power from the money she earned by writing. Still, Austen remembered what it was like to be poor and dependent when she created Fanny Price, and what it was like to be trapped by duty and dependence when she created Anne Elliot; but she also allowed herself to wonder how an heiress with no financial cares, Emma Woodhouse, occupied herself when just getting by is not an issue. Her last heroine, Charlotte Heywood of the unfinished *Sanditon*, was the anti-Emma: sensible, not rich, but comfortable; her parents were respectable country people with a large family. Where would Austen's pen have travelled had she lived longer? What works would she have produced as England entered the Victorian era and as the Industrial Revolution progressed? Would she have followed the example of Elizabeth Gaskell and Charles Dickens into social commentary? Perhaps, but it would have been Jane Austen-brand social commentary, witty and intelligent,

skewering her characters on a fine and very sharp spit, prepared for roasting and served up done to a turn.

As she wrote more books, and as her brand grew, Austen would no doubt have become richer as she grew older and her fame no doubt grew. Personal wealth would have given her some freedom to travel, but she was a homebody. She would likely have continued her retired life in Chawton with her sister Cassandra, her mother and Martha Lloyd – a matriarchy supportive of her art. Like some of her more fecund motherly characters, Austen would have birthed a goodly family of her "children", as she referred to her books more than once, and no doubt like the Morland family, there would have been literary heads and arms and legs enough for the number.

Sadly, Janeites cannot long indulge in the delightful fantasy of a dozen or more Jane Austen brand novels, for Austen did not live the three-score years and ten described in the Psalms; she barely made two-score. Jane made her sister Cassandra her literary executor – interestingly passing over her brother Henry – and she chose well. While Cassandra did not actively seek to publish her sister's work, she followed up on presented opportunities. Austen's work fell out of print from 1821, four years after her death, until 1832, when Richard

Bentley purchased the copyrights from Cassandra and Egerton's heirs and republished all six novels.

Cassandra took her job as literary executor seriously. She was careful to dispose of the books properly and also careful to get some money for herself, as Jane no doubt intended. She did her job so well that Jane Austen's books have never been out of print since.

So where does that leave us in these heady days, when books are available with the press of a button on the mobile phones we carry with us at all times, and when fans can engage with Jane Austen's work in entirely new ways? The question remains: what would Jane Austen have thought of the 21st-century version of the Jane Austen brand? I still don't like to presume. But considering her conduct as a professional author throughout her short career, I think Austen might have appreciated the ability for authors, many of them female, to make a bit of "pewter". And when stuff gets real for professional authors, it's all about the pewter. Jane Austen, the professional author, the businesswoman, certainly knew that, and I think she would have embraced – and possibly laughed at – those who dare to play in her sandbox two centuries later.

SOURCES

Austen, Jane. *Northanger Abbey*. Ed. R. W. Chapman. Oxford: OUP, 1988

Austen, Jane. *Minor Works*. Ed. R. W. Chapman. Oxford: OUP, 1988

Austen-Leigh, J. E. *A Memoir of Jane Austen and Other Family Recollections*. Oxford: OUP, 2002

Fergus, Jan. *Jane Austen: A Literary Life*. London: Macmillan Press, 1991

Le Faye, Deirdre, ed. *Jane Austen's Letters*. 4th Ed. Oxford: OUP, 2011

MARGARET C. SULLIVAN

Margaret C. Sullivan is the author of *The Jane Austen Handbook* and *Jane Austen Cover to Cover*. She is the founder of **austenblog.com** and also blogs at **habitofjournaling.com**

• • • • •

JANE AUSTEN'S LITERARY LEGACY

·····

EMILY BRAND discovers why Austen's writing has inspired novelists for two centuries

The first of Jane Austen's characters to receive a public outing were Elinor and Marianne Dashwood, with the publication of *Sense and Sensibility* in October 1811. The first edition was received with enough gentle praise to secure interest in her next offering, *Pride and Prejudice* – with this, her place among the writers of the day was assured. The dramatist Richard Brinsley Sheridan advised a friend to "buy it immediately, for it is one of the cleverest things", and Annabella Milbanke – the future Lady Byron – called it not only "a very superior work" but also "at present the fashionable novel".

Since then, changing tastes have led to Austen's fiction waxing in and out of fashion, and it has divided literary opinion – George Eliot and Virginia Woolf felt their debt to her, but Charlotte Brontë and Mark Twain were critical of the conventional world that she represented. Nevertheless, her creations have inspired generations of writers in countless ways – her legacy is inescapable and can be traced across continents and through the centuries. Most directly, her characters have been reimagined and her settings appropriated. Elements of her style have been imitated or vehemently reacted against. More generally, her stylistic innovations pushed English fiction into subtly experimental territories, and she has been credited with not only shaping what "Englishness" is in fiction, but also the development of literature on an international stage. Beyond the enduring popularity of *Pride and Prejudice*, *Emma* and *Persuasion* have been singled out as turning points in the evolution of the modern novel –

highlighting that the genius of Austen lies not only in her ability to create a world that so utterly absorbs readers, but also the originality of her voice.

Austen's identity as the author of her novels was not acknowledged in print until her obituary in July 1817 – despite rumours sparked by her loose-tongued brother – but they nonetheless created ripples in the world of fashionable literature. Some were superficial; on her own foray in fiction, Caroline Lamb pondered the title *Principle and Passion*, "since the fashion is to call every thing in the manner of Pride & prejudice, sense & sensibility". Others were more profound.

To many, these witty evocations of domestic life and love were a balm to the prevailing enthusiasm for sensational Gothic fiction. Missing the melodrama of Ann Radcliffe's novels, and deemed refreshingly inoffensive to the morals of the reading public, it was hoped that this style of fiction might drag literature into the realms of respectability. "No wind-howlings in long galleries; no drops of blood upon a rusty dagger – things that now should be left to ladies' maids and sentimental washer-women," wrote the critic William Gifford in 1815. The "smallness" and familiarity of her dramas also contrasted with sweeping historical fiction popularised by Byron and Walter Scott, steeped in Romanticism.

(Despite this difference in style, Scott, incidentally, later considered that "excellent lessons" could be learnt from Austen, who achieved "a finishing-off in some of her scenes that is really quite above everybody".) Though in this she was of course following in the footsteps of other authors, including Frances Burney and Maria Edgeworth, the reception of her novels encouraged a shift towards the everyday rather than the extraordinary. Many were directly inspired to update or even begin their own literary endeavours. The prolific author Mary Russell Mitford, writing between the 1810s and the 1850s,

IMAGE Walter Scott considered that "excellent lessons" could be learnt from some of Jane Austen's scenes

explained to a friend in 1825 that she intended to make her latest work a portrait of "common English life in the country, as playful, and as true, as I can make it, in other words, as like Miss Austen".

This was expressed more widely in the vogue for what became known as the "Silver Fork" novels of the 1820s and 1830s, which spoke to and satirised the manners of the upper classes. In its engagement with its particular subject matter this school of authors was evidently indebted to Austen, though

they didn't necessarily inherit her sharp eye or skill with characterisation. Unfortunately for the genre most were dismissed as crass and hackneyed, and though advertised as "by aristocrats, and for aristocrats", their appeal lay largely with the middle classes. Some authors, such as Lady Blessington and Charlotte Gore, profited considerably from the commercial success of their novels, but after the trend buckled in the 1840s their names were largely forgotten. Though they can be considered a bridge between Regency authors and the moralistic writers of the Victorian age, they remain a relatively neglected group.

However, Austen's early impact on the literary world ran deeper, though it might not be as immediately apparent. Two of her novels have been highlighted as particularly innovative in terms of style, form and tone – even as turning points in the development of English fiction. Professor John Mullan has suggested that, as a pioneer of a "free indirect style" of narration, *Emma* should be ranked alongside the radically experimental works of Flaubert, Joyce and Woolf. Presenting the action in the third person, but colouring the perspective with the thoughts and expressions of the fictional protagonist, Austen developed a distinct narrative voice. As such we share in our heroine's emotional responses, misguided assumptions and self-deceptions to an extent not found in earlier novels. In the more sombre and lyrical *Persuasion*, the critic Harold Bloom – like Virginia Woolf before him – locates Austen's "authenticity" as a writer in her movement away from the "Aristocratic" towards the "Democratic Age". Evidently, while her works went some way to moulding a public taste for small drama in high places, in these ways her experimentation with style also gently set literature on new tracks.

Into the Victorian age, there was relatively little interest in her work. The novels fell out of copyright and were increasingly considered quaint and old-fashioned. By the mid-19th century her work represented to some a mannered and stifled time, which they had happily consigned to history and ought not to be given a place in art. When encouraged in 1848 to read *Pride and Prejudice*, Charlotte Brontë replied that she was utterly uninspired by the book's "accurate, daguerrotype portrait of a commonplace face" and remarked on Austen in general that "the Passions are perfectly unknown to her". Though Brontë would probably grimace at the idea of having a literary debt to Austen, her influence on this later generation of writers can be found in their reaction *against* her fiction and imitations of it. Writing in 1861, the American Ralph Waldo Emerson also wondered at her success when the worlds she created were so constrained, so *English*, and without capacity for invention; as far as he could see, "never was life so pinched and narrow".

Of course, Jane Austen's talent was not entirely unappreciated. Emerson's critique was itself borne of his bemusement at "why people hold Miss Austen's novels at so high a rate". The literary critic George Henry Lewes considered her, unfashionably for 1852, "the greatest artist that has ever written". He found a fellow admirer in the woman with whom he would embroil himself in a scandalous affair, an editor and translator now known by the pseudonym she used for her novels – George Eliot. When she began writing her own fiction in 1857, Eliot immersed herself in re-reading Austen's work, suggesting that she certainly didn't count it among what she decried as frothy and damaging "Silly Novels by Lady Novelists". Though Eliot's own writing departed markedly in many ways – in exploration of unfamiliar settings, and a tendency to infuse her writing with moral and philosophical reflections – her engagement with Austen is reflected in her own mastery of social life in miniature, most strikingly in *Middlemarch*.

The protracted "Austen controversy" correspondence between Mary Russell Mitford and her friend Elizabeth Barrett Browning in the 1840s, debating the merits of Austen's "conformity" against the feverish imagination of others, enabled both to formulate their ideas about what constituted valuable literature. Here, as elsewhere, even while fashions steered in a new direction, Austen's legacy glimmered beneath the melodrama and adventure of Victorian fiction.

With the publication of an affectionate memoir of her life in 1869, and the ensuing "cult of the Divine Jane", Austen was thrust back into the spotlight. This first biography, written by her nephew James Edward Austen-Leigh, painted a pleasingly domestic and perfectly "feminine" portrait of the author bound to appeal to Victorian sensibilities – it did, and the first print

run sold out quickly. Her private letters were published in 1884 and demand for her novels surged, culminating with the beautiful editions illustrated by Hugh Thomson in the 1890s. As ever, this popularity stirred uncharitable thoughts in the bosoms of fellow writers – in 1898 Mark Twain attacked the "oppressive" Englishness that she now represented: "Every time I read *Pride and Prejudice* I want to dig her up and beat her over the skull with her own shin-bone," he wrote. But inevitably the heightened public appreciation encouraged writers to reconsider her significance – even if the figure now

IMAGE Virginia Woolf said that she felt her own debt to Jane Austen

held in such high regard was veiled in myths cultivated by her nephew.

Although this burst of what might now be termed "fandom" subsided into the 1900s, interest in Austen was by now entrenched in English culture. In reading, re-reading and contemplating Austen, innumerable authors – male and female – have absorbed her as part of their mental landscape. In the 1920s Virginia Woolf turned repeatedly to the subject, feeling her own debt to Austen keenly but also crediting her with the professionalism and powers of innovation that she had been stripped of during the cult of "the Divine Jane". In scrutinising her methods of composition Woolf found something similar to her own, and speculated that when Austen died aged 42 – "the height of her powers" – she was on the verge of undertaking a stylistic "voyage of discovery" that would have secured her a quite different reputation. On the surface it may seem unlikely that the acerbic playwright Samuel Beckett could have owed her much, yet he wrote to a friend in 1935: "I think she has much to teach me." In *The Great Tradition* (1948), which explored the meaning of the novel in a world recovering from the catastrophe of war, the literary critic F. R. Leavis named Jane Austen as one of four "great English novelists". As controversial as it may have been for him to present this (very)

select canon so badly, it is difficult to argue with his statement that Austen is "a major fact in the background of other writers".

One of the most obvious 20th-century descendants of Austen, though perhaps not quite in the way that Leavis meant, is Georgette Heyer. In a writing career spanning 50 years, she is best known for the Regency romances credited with establishing the genre. Though her work lacks the originality and satirical intent of Austen, it is undeniably derivative of her written style, themes, setting and (on occasion) plot lines. From Heyer's first novel in this style, *Regency Buck* (1935), they were devoured by a readership wanting more of Austen's world and tapped into a nostalgia that continues to flourish in print and online today.

The astounding success of adaptations for film and television, most notably those of the 1990s, marked the advent of a second "Austenmania". (Somewhat bizarrely, in 1996 *Vanity Fair* proclaimed that Jane Austen was "the hottest writer in showbusiness".) Inevitably, this rediscovery of the novels has given rise to a diverse and bewildering array of fiction appropriating or reimagining her characters in new circumstances, environments and eras. Many rely on the Austen association but others, such as Helen Fielding's *Bridget Jones's Diary*

(1996), construct a thoroughly modern novel around the bare bones of Austen, scattering it with tributes and allusions to its inheritance.

Austen's presence can also be felt more subtly in the fiction of the postwar era, in England as per Leavis's study, but also around the world. In 1964, four years after the publication of *To Kill a Mockingbird*, Harper Lee quipped in a radio interview: "All I want to be is the Jane Austen of South Alabama." However half-serious Lee was, the lineage is evident in her exploration of social patterns in close-knit community, of coming-of-age, and in her sideways glances at snobbery. In 2015 Salman Rushdie wrote of Austen's influence on modern Anglo-Indian literature, giving a similar picture of how her underlying values and themes effortlessly transcend time and place. As sharp examinations of matrimonial and familial interactions, he highlighted Anita Desai's *Clear Light of Day* (1980) and Vikram Seth's *A Suitable Boy* (1993) as clear descendants of the literary tradition that Austen played a major role in developing. She is an exemplar of writing the world of women "brimming with potential

but doomed by narrow convention to an interminable *Huis-clos* of ballroom dancing and husband hunting" – a world applicable to Regency England or post-partition India.

It would be impossible to survey the true reaches of Jane Austen's literary legacy, even with a lifetime of research. Admiration of her work has shaped the literary direction that some have taken, and inspired others to pick up a pen in the first place. She has acted as a marker against which countless writers have negotiated and formulated their own identities and styles, whether they valued her or quite the opposite. In mass-market fiction, for the worlds she recreated so succinctly and courtship themes, she has been held up as the mother of the Regency romance novel. Perhaps owing to her unnuanced Victorian reputation as an ideal feminine writer – unassuming but amusing, concerned with the "trivial" themes of love and marriage – she also has a place in the ancestry of "chick lit".

The effects of Austen's ingenuity in so many different elements of her work echo through the evolution of literary fiction, through the 19th and 20th centuries and beyond. In her powers of social and psychological observation, her experimentation with new forms of expression and characterisation, her confident embrace of domestic themes, her masterful comic voice, the timelessness of the values at the heart of her novels: all entered and added new colour to the literary landscape. In the realm of Literature (with a capital 'L'), all writers have a debt to Austen, whether they would care to recognise it or not.

EMILY BRAND

Emily Brand is a writer and historian with a special interest in romantic relationships during the long eighteenth century: **emilybrand.co.uk**

• • • • •

IMAGE Harper Lee, the American novelist, once said: "All I want to be is the Jane Austen of South Alabama"

HER LEGACY TO NOVELISTS

· · · · ·

There are lessons for all novelists in Jane Austen's work, as **CARRIE BEBRIS** explains

In January 1817, at age 41, Jane Austen began writing what would become her final novel. The manuscript, untitled by Austen but known today as *Sanditon* for its eponymous fictional setting, was set aside two months later and remained unfinished upon her death.

Some 195 years later, I began a formal apprenticeship with Jane Austen. Although I did not make the connection at the time, like Austen, I had recently entered my forties. Like Austen, I had already written a number of novels, preceded by juvenilia of varying length and theme. (However, unlike Austen's, my juvenilia is not held in the collections of major world libraries, but reside in an unassuming box in my basement, sharing a shelf with Christmas gift wrap and a bowling ball that I haven't used in at least two decades.) Also at the time, I did not think of the journey on which I was about to embark as an apprenticeship. After all, when entering such a relationship, generally both the master and the student are alive, and one of us was deficient in that condition.

But the magical thing about the written word is its ability to transcend time and space, to reach across oceans and centuries to entertain, enlighten and empower readers whom the author never imagined she or he would address. The most humbling and gratifying moments of my career have not been the public affirmations of awards and starred reviews (though, admittedly, those are nice too). Rather,

IMAGE Georgette Heyer is one of the most popular writers to have inherited the Austen legacy

they have come in the form of the quieter voices of readers who have told me how one of my books touched their lives – provided succour, or humour, or escape when they needed it.

Jane Austen's words have been doing that for two centuries. Moreover, she has inspired some of her readers to become novelists themselves. And for those who pay close attention, she has provided instruction.

Anyone who has wandered the aisles (or web pages) of a bookstore in the past decade or so cannot be insensible of the fact that Jane Austen has evolved from being merely one of the world's greatest authors to having become a genre unto herself. Where once upon a time, Austen-related books were mostly limited to biography,

literary criticism and Georgian social history – while fiction inspired by her works largely took the form of Regency romances by Georgette Heyer and other romance novelists – today's library offers a seemingly endless array of sequels, prequels, variations, pastiches, modern retellings, "inspired by" stories, completions, spin-offs, mash-ups and stories in which Austen herself appears as a character; they span genres ranging from historical fiction, romance and mystery to picture books, middle grade/young adult, paranormal, time-travel, erotica and horror.

Although most of my own novels fall under the Austenesque umbrella, I never set out to write an Austen sequel. Having previously published two fantasy novels, I discovered that I preferred writing battle scenes fought with rapier wit rather than with actual rapiers, and thought that the mystery genre might be a better fit for the type of conflict I wanted to explore. So I set out to write the sort of mysteries I most enjoy as a reader or viewer: those with some kind of literary connection, and those with an amateur sleuth – preferably a couple (already or not yet romantically involved) who engage in clever banter as they step around the bodies. Austen had long been my favorite author, so a literary connection that somehow involved her or her works was a natural choice.

I considered numerous premises – some historical, some contemporary, some set in the real world, others in the worlds of her characters. During this generative period, I re-read *Pride and Prejudice,* and when I reached the crisis of Lydia's elopement, I was struck by how Elizabeth – described by Mr Bingley earlier in the novel as a "studier of character" – predicts Lydia's fall and warns their father of the imprudence of allowing Lydia to go to Brighton, while Darcy, as a man of the world with connections and resources, is able to move about London following the clues in his possession until he locates the errant couple and brings Mr Wickham to heel. I thought that if their strengths and talents could complement each other's that well before they got together romantically, imagine what they could accomplish after.

I had found my sleuthing couple – and a premise for not merely a single book, but a series. Darcy and Elizabeth would be the Nick and Nora Charles of Regency England, reluctant investigators who come to the aid of family and friends who find themselves embroiled in intrigue, engaging in their signature repartee as they meet characters from other Austen novels and solve plots woven with threads Austen left behind.

I have been writing the *Mr & Mrs Darcy* Mystery series for more than 15 years now. Austen has been a tremendous influence not only in the most obvious sense (the premises and plots of my stories), but also on my creative process, and even how I view myself as a writer. It is an influence that, especially in hindsight, I recognise in myself and in works I wrote long before the *Mr & Mrs Darcy* series was conceived. Though my formal apprenticeship (what I mean by that, I will explain shortly) began in 2011, I was receiving indirect lessons from Austen from the time I first read her as a teenager.

Most writers begin as voracious readers and in the process of consuming work after work we subconsciously absorb many elements of our craft. We might not be able to articulate what we've learnt about pacing or character development, but we recognise how successfully (or not) it is done in the works of others and we strive to do it well in our own. With experience and more active study of the craft we become more adept at honing these elements in our own novels, and more conscious of them in others' novels. It is a rare event when I can lose myself in a book the way I could when I was ten – half my brain cannot help but analyse the writing and structure.

In reading Jane Austen throughout my teenage and young adult years, I was reading the best, passively

IMAGE Colin Firth starred as Mr Darcy

internalising the writing lessons hidden in plain sight within her novels. When I started writing the *Mr & Mrs Darcy* mysteries, I read each of her novels more closely than ever before, alert not only to macro craft and story issues, but also the tiniest details of characters, settings and plots – looking for loose threads, potential clues, character histories and other details that would help me to maintain continuity between my novels and those of Austen.

So it was that, upon finishing my sixth *Mr & Mrs Darcy* Mystery (*The Deception at Lyme*), I was faced with the question of where to take the Darcys next. I had written one mystery inspired

by each of Austen's six published novels. When I resolved to go where Jane Austen had gone after completing *Persuasion* – to the fictional village of Sanditon – I decided that it was also time for a more intensive study of her writing process.

Until that time I had read Austen's finished products – her novels as they appeared in print. Even Austen's juvenilia and minor works that exist only in manuscript form, I had read in typeset editions edited by scholars and published by university presses. Someone else had read through the handwritten pages for me – discerned the cramped insertions, excised the cross-outs, judged whether that character was an "o" or an "a" and therefore what word resulted; written out abbreviations, added paragraph breaks and cleaned up punctuation to make the text more visually friendly to modern eyes. Though the editors were notable professionals, they were nevertheless filters.

This time I wanted to see Austen's process without a third party interpreting it for me. And so my formal apprenticeship began. In the quiet of winter, I read the *Sanditon* manuscript in Austen's own hand. Word by word, I created my own transcription, immersing myself in her writing in a way that I had never experienced before. It was the closest

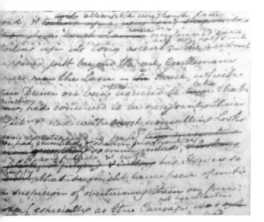

IMAGE The handwritten manuscript of *Sanditon* is not the easiest to read

that one can come to seeing her process in action. Her handwriting is not the easiest to read, particularly on pages with insertions and crossed-out text – the ones of greatest interest to me as I speculated about her reason for substituting one sentence or word for another. But each day I became more fluent, and when I reached the final page I was sorry to transcribe the last word.

Jane Austen did not reveal a secret that makes the monumental work of writing a novel as effortless as her finished books make it appear; one was not encoded for posterity in the handwritten lines of her final manuscript, nor did she send me a message from the Great Beyond. Nevertheless, by the end I felt that we had been on a journey together – she the

master, I the apprentice, eager to absorb whatever wisdom she was able to offer. Even among authors who don't work with her text so intimately, Austen is still a mentor, particularly to women writers. Here are some of the lessons she teaches:

It is possible to write good novels despite the demands that others place upon you

Whenever I visit Chawton Cottage I am struck by both the size and location of Austen's writing table. It is incredible to me that she wrote some of the greatest works of world literature on a table barely large enough to hold paper and ink, in the common sitting room where she depended upon a creaking door hinge to herald the imminent entrance of visitors in enough time to cover up what she was writing. I find it difficult enough to compose with my family anywhere in the house.

Life is full of people and responsibilities that claim our time and attention, and our present age of instant communication has made interruptions even more frequent. Virginia Woolf, in *A Room of One's Own*, suggests that female writers were – and still are – drawn to the novel as their chosen literary form because it can sustain the inevitable interruptions that will occur during its composition. It is easier to return to a novel and resume work after a forced break of hours, days or years, than to return to other literary forms.

Jane Austen suffered interruptions every day of her writing life. Find a way to close the door (literally if you can, figuratively if not) on your most common interruptions, and write until the squeaky hinge demands that you stop.

Make the most of whatever writing time you have

In the eight weeks that Jane worked on the *Sanditon* manuscript, she wrote eleven and a half chapters totalling some 24,800 words – about a fifth to a third of the length of one of her published novels.

Eight weeks – during which she was subjected to not only the usual interruptions just described, but also the discomfort and distraction of failing health. Never knowing how soon she would have to lay aside her pen, she wrote what she could, when she could. Your writing time is precious. Guard it jealously, even if it comes in spurts, and do not allow distractions to intrude until you can no longer hold them at bay.

Find your writer's voice

In an 1816 letter to her nephew, himself an aspiring writer, Austen expresses sympathy for the disappearance of two and a half chapters of his work-in-progress. She then jokes:

> It is well that I have not been at Steventon lately, & therefore cannot be suspected of purloining them . . . I do not think however that any theft of that sort would really be very useful to me. What should I do with your strong, manly, spirited Sketches, full of Variety & Glow? – How could I possibly join them on to the little bit (two Inches wide) of Ivory on which I work with so fine a Brush, as produces little effect after much labour?[1]

Austen understood that each author possesses a unique voice, and that to attempt imitation or grafting one on to another would sound inauthentic, undermining the power of the story. Find *your* voice. Develop it. And trust it to tell *your* stories.

Do not give up on a story that you believe in

Sense and Sensibility, Pride and Prejudice and *Northanger Abbey* all underwent major revision years after their original composition. Although some manuscripts are better abandoned, others are worth the effort of re-vision: seeing your work again with fresh eyes after time has granted you some distance.

Stay true to your own vision and strengths

Among the most wryly amusing pieces

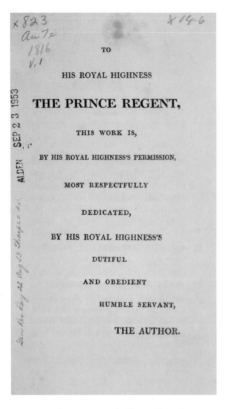

TO

HIS ROYAL HIGHNESS

THE PRINCE REGENT,

THIS WORK IS,

BY HIS ROYAL HIGHNESS'S PERMISSION,

MOST RESPECTFULLY

DEDICATED,

BY HIS ROYAL HIGHNESS'S

DUTIFUL

AND OBEDIENT

HUMBLE SERVANT,

THE AUTHOR.

IMAGE *Emma* was dedicated to the Prince Regent at his request

of Austen's surviving correspondence is a series of letters between her and the Rev James Stanier Clarke, librarian to the Prince Regent. After Clarke escorted Austen through Carlton House (the Prince's London residence), Austen sought clarification on whether a statement he had made during her visit – that she was at liberty to dedicate any future work to the Prince – meant that she was obliged to dedicate *Emma*, which was currently in the press. He replied that while it was not incumbent upon her to dedicate anything to the Prince, should she wish to do so, she had permission. Austen was fluent enough at reading between the lines to recognise that, regardless of her poor opinion of the Prince, accepting this unsolicited permission was in her best interest.

Their correspondence might have ended there. However, Clarke was as much an admirer of Austen's novels as was the Prince Regent and demonstrated his exuberance by generously offering her several ideas for the subjects of future novels. He twice suggested clergymen (who happened to be remarkably similar to himself) as protagonists. Austen gently declined. After being appointed chaplain and private English Secretary to Leopold, Prince of Coburg (who had recently become engaged to Princess Charlotte, the Prince Regent's daughter), Clarke next suggested:

> *Perhaps when you again appear in print you may chuse to dedicate your Volumes to Prince Leopold: any Historical Romance illustrative of the History of the august house of Cobourg, would just now be very interesting.*[2]

Again, Austen tactfully declined, citing

as obstacles her own shortcomings. Though Clarke now had connections to two powerful men, Austen nevertheless chose artistic integrity over profit, saying: "I could no more write a Romance than an Epic Poem ... I must keep to my own style & go on in my own Way."[3]

Your experience is the source of the universal truths that will come out in your stories

> You are now collecting your People delightfully, getting them exactly into such a spot as is the delight of my life; – 3 or 4 Families in a Country Village is the very thing to work on.[4]

Austen offered those words of advice in 1814 to Anna Austen, her 21-year-old niece, in a letter devoted almost entirely to constructive criticism of a book manuscript that the aspiring novelist had sent her aunt for review. Jane wrote about what she knew, and it is that deep knowledge of her subject that makes her stories and characters resonate with truth. Her fictional "People" seem real because they *are* real – we have met them before in our own lives.

Collect your People. Get them into a spot that is the delight of *your* life. Then write them and their story as honestly as you can.

SOURCES

1 Letter to James Edward Austen, December 17, 1816

2 Letter to James Stanier Clarke, March 27, 1816

3 April 1, 1816

4 Letter to Anna Austen, September 18, 1814

CARRIE BEBRIS

Carrie Bebris is author of the *Mr & Mrs Darcy* Mystery series in which the married Elizabeth Bennet and Mr Darcy from Jane Austen's *Pride and Prejudice* become entangled in intrigue with other Austen characters: **carriebebris.com**

• • • • •

CLOSER TO JANE

· · · · ·

Many Austen fans enjoy re-creating and re-enacting the Regency world in which the author lived, writes **KIM WILSON**

The story of Pride and Prejudice *has of late years become known to a constantly, almost rapidly, increasing cult, as it must be called, for the readers of Jane Austen are hardly ever less than her adorers: she is a passion and a creed, if not quite a religion.* – William Dean Howells, *Heroines of Fiction*, 1901

Jane Austen's ardent devotees of the late 19th and early 20th centuries would no doubt have been pleased to learn that by the beginning of the 21st century the number of her passionate followers had increased exponentially and that this enthusiasm showed no signs of waning, even 200 years after her death. Jane Austen and her novels are more popular today than ever before. She is the subject of fan clubs, blogs, literary societies and even a magazine, all dedicated to the study and enjoyment of the author, her books and her world.

The explosive rise in the numbers of Jane Austen fans and Regency re-enactors seems to be directly attributable to the popularity of the many new filmed versions of Austen's novels, beginning with the 1995 BBC series *Pride and Prejudice* that starred Jennifer Ehle as Elizabeth Bennet and Colin Firth as Mr Darcy. Many of the earlier film versions of the novels had been popular enough, but the fervour with which fans greeted the

IMAGE Jennifer Ehle and Colin Firth starred in the 1995 *Pride and Prejudice*

smouldering on-screen chemistry between Ehle and Firth passed all previous boundaries. The moment when Firth emerges from a swim in the lake at "Pemberley", wet shirt plastered to his well-muscled torso (a scene that appears nowhere in the novel) sealed the appeal of Austen's stories as stand-alone filmed versions whose popularity might now be independent of an

> 'This movie gave me tremendous hope and fed my soul'

appreciation for Austen's literary talent in book form. Other popular Austen-inspired films soon followed.

Fans now had vivid, more or less accurate representations (depending on the filmmaker) of the world of Austen's characters, and they were eager to copy what they saw. Toni Tumbusch, a Jane Austen Society of North America member and an avid Regency re-enactor, admits that she came to Jane Austen via the movies that were released in the mid-1990s, primarily Emma Thompson's *Sense and Sensibility*: "It came out at an extremely vulnerable period in my life … and this movie both gave me tremendous hope and fed my soul. This led me to the books, which led me to English Country Dancing,

which led me to the Jane Austen Society, which in turn led me to Regency period re-enacting. And to think that something which led to such a big part of my life began with just a movie."

Many modern Janeites (a term whose origins date as far back as 1894) delight in re-enacting the Regency. They array themselves in Regency dresses and finery or dashing military uniforms, take part in Regency dances, cook Regency food, play Regency games, and learn lost Regency skills, all to re-create and understand the world of Jane Austen as they imagine it must have been. Few authenticated possessions of Jane Austen herself have survived to the present day, so those that do exist hold a special place in the imaginations of her followers. Several are on display at her Chawton Cottage home in Hampshire (now known as Jane Austen's House Museum) and are eagerly re-created by her admirers to the best of their abilities.

They sew themselves pelisses (a type of coat) similar to that thought to have been worn by Austen; weave beaded bracelets like her delicate, lacy blue and white flowered one; search auction websites for antique topaz and gold crosses like those her brother Charles gave to her and her sister, Cassandra; and commission

IMAGE Jane Austen's turquoise ring

jewellers to make copies of her simple gold and turquoise ring that recently came to light. Austen's turquoise blue ring, her bracelet in which blue is the predominant colour, and her blue dress in her watercolour portrait painted by Cassandra have even caused some of Austen's admirers to conjecture whether blue could have been her favourite colour. From such small things, "two strong twigs & a half towards a Nest" (an expression she uses in a letter of December 16, 1816, to a favorite nephew) Janeites build a speculative picture of Jane Austen's preferences and taste and so come closer, they hope, to understanding her better.

Many carry on beyond Austen's real, historical world, extending their passion into the imaginary worlds of her novels. What, they wonder, would life at Norland Park, Hartfield, Longbourne, or even Pemberley have been like?

How would Marianne Dashwood or Anne Elliot have dressed? What did the rout cakes in *Emma* taste like? Was life aboard Captain Wentworth's ships as difficult and dangerous as we suspect? And what were the names of the dances that Elizabeth and Darcy danced together at the Netherfield Ball? It says much for the authenticity and timeless appeal of the characters Austen created that so many Janeites are happy to spend endless hours talking and debating not only the nature of the characters themselves (Mrs Bennet: good mother or bad?), but also how they would have lived, what clothing they would have worn, and what activities and pastimes they would have engaged in, all as if they were historical figures.

There is a large overlap between those who are interested in re-enacting the Regency because they love Jane Austen and those who re-enact because they love some particular historical period or historical activity. For almost any historical Regency activity there is a research or re-enacting group devoted to studying and/or re-creating the best, most accurate interpretation of it. There are re-enacting and historical research groups who examine Regency life in general, and also highly specialised groups who study such diverse activities as historic cooking, hairdressing, military re-enactment, gardening, costuming and dance. The groups'

IMAGE A Regency re-enactor at the Jane Austen Festival in Bath

social media sites are populated with like-minded individuals who clearly delight in talking to each other about the finer points of understanding and re-creating the Regency. On one site members ask each other for tips on how many yards of fabric are needed for a Regency riding habit; on another, members debate whether sausage-roll hair curls are possible without adding artificial hair; on a third, members discuss the proper food to cook at a military camp re-enactment; and on yet another members cheerfully thrash out the finer points of what type of hat would have been worn by a gentleman in the rain in the north of England in the summer of 1816.

Tumbusch's husband, Tom, is also a Jane Austen Society of North America member and an enthusiastic Regency re-enactor. Both are passionate about experiential history. Toni is an accomplished costumer, writes an elegant hand with nibbed and quill pens, and is wickedly accurate at Regency archery. Tom portrays the 3rd lieutenant of HMS *Acasta*, a British naval ship circa 1800-10 "for the educational benefit of the public and for the mutual research and enjoyment of the individual members". Both are historic dance instructors. Together, their interests exemplify the broad range of Regency re-enactment possibilities. "I view Regency re-enacting as a means to get closer to Jane" said Toni. "I find that immersing myself in the material culture of the period helps me to know her better . . . Pursuing Regency era re-enacting has . . . entailed doing a lot of research into the lifestyles, customs and clothing of the time, and then setting about to re-create these things. It is difficult to describe the sensation of donning period types of clothing and gathering with likeminded and like-garbed people in some re-creation of a Regency period event. There is a certain magic that happens, and when this magic happens to cross over into a Jane Austen event, the magic is heightened, for then you have an additional and meaningful element that brings you together."

Austen's modern fans often comment that they like re-enacting the Regency period and re-creating the physical aspects of its world because they are attracted to what seems to them to be a simpler time, quieter and more restful than their hectic modern world. Life was more elegant, too, they say, perhaps thinking more of the gaieties of the Netherfield Ball in *Pride and Prejudice* than of the squalid and difficult lives of the cottagers in *Emma* and *Mansfield Park*. At balls, most re-enactors choose to dress up as the gentry and aristocrats of Austen's era – there are remarkably few volunteers to dress as the scrubby, desperate poor. Such imaginings seem to have a wistful quality to them. There is the sense that perhaps we Janeites feel that by acquiring or re-creating the goods and pastimes of Jane Austen's era we can transmute the base metal of our modern lives into the noble gold of a mythical past by an almost alchemical process.

Regardless of whether or not such expectations are realistic, our choices in the world of historical re-enactment often have a deeply personal emotional resonance. Jane Austen's modern devotees often describe that the experiential aspects of re-enacting or re-creating the same pastimes and activities and even the objects found in Austen's books and the Austen-inspired movies give them a feeling of connection to her characters and indeed, they think, to Austen herself. When we give a Regency-style tea party, sipping Bohea tea from delicate china cups and enjoying rich slices of plum cake, we imagine ourselves perhaps taking tea with Emma: "They sat down to tea – the same party round the same table – how often it had been collected! – and how often had her eyes fallen on the same shrubs in the lawn, and observed the same beautiful effect of the western sun!"

When we plan our attire for a Regency ball and carefully choose the muslins for our replica gowns – sprigged, spotted, or tamboured? blue trimmings or green? – we feel a kinship with Catherine Morland in *Northanger Abbey*, who lies awake debating which dress she should wear for the next assembly, with "nothing but the shortness of the time prevent[ing] her buying a new one for the evening", in the hopes that Henry Tilney will think she once again appears "to much advantage". Toni Tumbusch agrees: "Eventually, following these re-enacting pursuits made me feel like I was in one of the many wonderful Jane Austen movies. If I was at an English country dance, I felt like I was in a ballroom scene. If I was doing period archery with my English longbow and self-nocked arrows, it was as if I was in the Gwyneth Paltrow and Jeremy Northam version of *Emma*. And when I sat down to write a letter with my nibbed pen, a bottle of ink, a writing desk, and sealing wax, I felt like I was Elizabeth writing to her dear sister Jane in *Pride and Prejudice*, or perhaps I was even Jane Austen herself!"

Some literature professors and other practitioners of literary criticism, accustomed as they are to approaching Austen and her texts solely from a literary perspective, seem at times uneasy, even disapproving, of this intersection of literature, history and fandom. However, others maintain that experiential history (even enthusiastic variations thereof) enhances readers' understanding of the social realities that Austen experienced and that must necessarily have informed her work. Natasha Duquette, in her essay

IMAGE Toni and Tom Tumbusch are avid Regency re-enactors

Laughter over Tea: Jane Austen and Culinary Pedagogy, explains how she and her students held teas, including preparing and serving historically accurate Regency food, and how those experiences enhanced their understanding of the texts. She adds: "The Jane Austen tea, then, helps us become more aware of how Austen uses tea-time to generate and sustain humour, sympathy, familial love and romantic attachment among her characters." By engaging the past through such hands-on activities, Duquette's students seemed not only to understand Jane Austen's works better, but to come into a shared community with each other, as one of the students, Emily Hollingshead, noted (quoted in Duquette): "There seems to be something about Jane Austen that gives us permission to be a little silly: to dress up for a picnic; to eat strange-looking food because it's what Elizabeth Bennet might have eaten; to rehash the debate between this and that movie adaptation for the 14th time; and at our third Jane Austen tea, with Emma Webster's *Lost in Austen*, to try our own hands at plotting the stories of Austen's heroines. That freedom in community is one of the things I love best about reading Jane Austen."

Tom Tumbusch agrees with that sentiment: "Experiential learning is part of the appeal of re-enacting, whether you're teaching history, learning about it, or both. It's one thing to read Jane's novels and other books about her time. It's quite another to put on the clothing of the period and re-create their way of life. It captures the imagination in a way that is often more compelling than the dry pages of a history textbook. You discover things that wouldn't be as easy to learn from books, such as how clothing affects the way you move, what food tastes like when you're limited to the ingredients and spices that were available at that time and place in history, or what it takes to make something by hand that you would casually buy at [a supermarket] today.

Educational and cultural institutions routinely use experiential learning as part of their standard curricula or offerings on the Regency era. Jane Austen's House Museum and Chawton House Library, housed in what was Jane Austen's brother Edward's house in the same village, collaborate to offer hands-on programmes to schools. Visiting students participate in writing workshops and tour the houses, but are also given the opportunity to dress in period costume, handle "real and replica objects", attend other workshops "relating to dress, manners and use of herbs" and even practise dancing at Chawton House "in replica clothes".

Hands-on, experiential Regency history has also spread to commercial

IMAGE Caroline Austen remembered the delightful times with "Aunt Jane"

ventures, encouraged perhaps by the many Austen-inspired costume dramas and such popular reality shows as *A Regency House Party,* where contestants spent a summer living under conditions meant to approximate the daily life of the gentry of Jane Austen's era. Some manor houses now offer paying guests the chance to fulfil their fantasies of living, for a weekend at least, at Pemberley. For example, Kentchurch Court, the site of *A Regency House Party,* promises that their costumed guests will "relive the splendour of Regency England" with "Regency dinners, music, literature, gossip, recital, cards and entertainments", as well as "reliving the

TV series whilst enjoying high society life".

Aware, perhaps, of the disapproval from some in literary criticism circles, some Janeites who choose to dress in Regency garb and re-enact Regency activities find themselves feeling slightly apologetic for their own enthusiasm. They go out of their way to assure others that they indeed value Austen's works as literature and are not to be classed as mere movie fans who pant over Colin Firth. Perhaps the more important question is not what literature professors think of costumed Austen fans, but rather what would Jane Austen herself think of the legions of her devotees who not only read her works, but also do their best to dress and act like her and her characters? Costumed Janeites can take comfort from the fact that Jane Austen herself was known to approve of the pleasant activity of dressing-up. Caroline Austen, one of her nieces, remembered the delightful times she and her cousins had visiting their beloved Aunt Jane: "When staying at Chawton, if my two cousins, Mary Jane and Cassy were there, we often had amusements in which my Aunt was very helpful . . . She would furnish us with what we wanted from her wardrobe, and *she* would often be the entertaining visitor in our make believe house – She amused us in various ways."

Not only did Jane Austen approve, but she indulged in dressing-up herself, as another niece, Fanny Knight, recorded in her diary for June 26, 1805: "Aunts and Grandmama played at school with us. Aunt Cassandra was Mrs. Teachum the Governess Aunt Jane, Miss Popham the Teacher Aunt Harriet, Sally the Housemaid, Miss Sharpe, the Dancing master the Apothecary and the Serjeant, Grandmama Betty Jones the Pie woman, and Mama the Bathing woman. They dressed in Character and we had a most delightful day."

While reading Jane Austen's novels gives some of her fans a feeling of a closeness to Austen's characters, reading her surviving letters, most of which were written to her sister, Cassandra, leads other devotees to feel as if they are almost honorary Austen family members, that they have been admitted to the privilege of being a part of her private life. Austen's most ardent admirers commonly say that they feel as if they perhaps could be her cousins, or possibly her nieces. Indeed, we Janeites hope that Austen (who always maintained the importance of aunts) would understand and even welcome our dressing up and mimicry with the indulgence of a fond aunt, knowing that we only want to be closer to her.

WORKS CITED

Austen, Caroline. *My Aunt Jane Austen, a Memoir*. Alton: Jane Austen Society, 1952.

Austen, Jane. *Letters*. Deirdre Le Faye, ed. Oxford: Oxford University Press, 2011.

Duquette, Natasha Aleksiuk. 'Laughter over Tea: Jane Austen and Culinary Pedagogy'. *Persuasions On-Line* 29. Jane Austen Society of North America, 2008.

Howells, William Dean. 'Jane Austen's Elizabeth Bennet'. *Heroines of Fiction ... With Illustrations by H.C. Christy, A.I. Keller, Etc.* Harper Bros.: London & New York, 1901.

Le Faye, Deirdre *Fanny Knight's Diaries*. 2000.

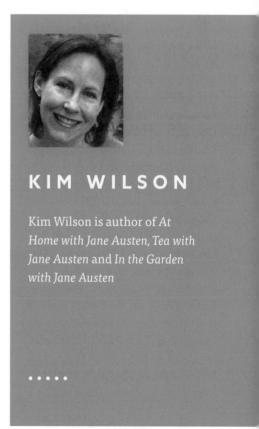

KIM WILSON

Kim Wilson is author of *At Home with Jane Austen, Tea with Jane Austen* and *In the Garden with Jane Austen*

. . . . .

PILGRIMS' PROGRESS

• • • • •

From Bath to Winchester and from Chawton to Lyme, an entire tourism industry has grown up around Jane Austen's legacy. **SUSANNAH FULLERTON** follows the Austen trail from 1867 until the present day

I n 1867 Alfred Lord Tennyson went on a walking tour in the West Country. On August 23 he walked nine miles from Bridport to Lyme, "led on to Lyme by the description of the place in Miss Austen's *Persuasion*", according to the memoir written by his son Hallam. Once in Lyme, Tennyson called on his friend Francis Palgrave, of *Golden Treasury* fame, and was shown around the town by various dignitaries. But there was only one thing that mattered to Tennyson. "Now take me to the Cobb and show me the steps from which Louisa Musgrove fell", he demanded. Those steps (and of course he could not even be sure which steps Jane Austen had had in mind) were much more real to him than sites connected with the landing of the Duke of Monmouth (whose ill-fated rebellion began from Lyme), more thrilling than any actual

historical events connected with the once thriving harbour town. *Persuasion* exerted a power over Tennyson's imagination far more urgent than did any "real solemn history". The power of Jane Austen's fiction did not touch Tennyson alone – the great Victorian poet would be amazed at the range, variety, financial impact and international reach of the Jane Austen tourism business today.

When *Pride and Prejudice* was published the playwright Richard Brinsley Sheridan was one of its first readers. At every dinner party he attended for some time he raved about this new novel. At that time there was little else for a fan to do but enthuse. Nobody then knew who the "Lady" was

IMAGE The Cobb at Lyme, where Louisa Musgrove fell, has been on the Austen trail since at least 1867

"Oh God! her father and mother!"
Chapter XII

I

who had written the book or where she lived, so an admirer could do little in the way of sightseeing. However, once word leaked out (thanks to Jane's proud brother Henry, who loved to boast of his clever sister's work), fans of the novels began to move. One woman who was encouraged to read *Pride and Prejudice* after hearing Sheridan praise it, began to travel regularly through Chawton in the hope that her carriage would obligingly break down so she could meet the author.

When Jane Austen died, admirers of her books started to visit Winchester Cathedral to see her grave and pay their respects there. By the 1860s, only 40 years after her death, there were so many pilgrims seeking out the grave, that the cathedral verger was puzzled. "Was there anything particular about that lady" he inquired. "So many people want to know where she was buried." It is hardly surprising that he was puzzled – the gravestone fails to mention the six published novels Jane Austen wrote. In 1900 a stained glass memorial window to Jane Austen was installed in the cathedral – it does not add further information concerning the novels, but it added to the growing sense that the grave was a shrine. This was enough for

IMAGE The house at 4 Sydney Place, Bath, photographed c1890, where Jane Austen lived from 1801 to 1805

Rudyard Kipling, who went out of his way to visit whenever he was in the area and who called Jane Austen's burial site "the holiest place in England".

In Bath, readers of *Northanger Abbey* and *Persuasion* walked the streets to find where Mrs Smith lodged, where Sir Walter resided on shaky ground and where Catherine Morland stayed with the Allens. Jane Austen's skilled use of the topography of that city meant that a tourist could walk exactly where the characters walked, shop where they shopped and admire the same views of Bath. But there was no "shrine" to visit in that city for those first Jane Austen pilgrims.

In 1870 James Edward Austen-Leigh, Jane's nephew, published his *Memoir of Jane Austen*, giving the first full account of her life and providing also illustrations of places connected with her life – the parsonage and the manor house at Steventon, and the church at Chawton. In some ways this was a very early and very rough guidebook to Jane Austen sites. In 1891 *The Story of Jane Austen's Life* by Oscar Fay Adams gave personal descriptions of places associated with her childhood, adulthood and death, and (in its second edition) provided photographs showing what condition houses and buildings associated with her were in by 1889. Tourists could now, thanks to such pictures, plan their own Jane Austen

JANE AUSTEN'S HOME

TO THE EDITOR OF THE TIMES

Sir,—We ask the hospitality of your columns, believing that many of your readers would be interested to hear of the existence of the Jane Austen Society and its aims. This society was founded in May, 1940, with the object of getting possession of the house formerly known as Chawton Cottage. In this house Jane Austen lived with her mother and her sister Cassandra from 1809 until her death in 1817. All the novels except " Northanger Abbey " were written here in the form in which we have them.

The cottage, besides being of unique interest to lovers of Jane Austen's work, is well worth preserving in itself. It is an L-shaped brick building of early Georgian date, standing at the junction of the London, Winchester, and Portsmouth roads. A description of it in Jane Austen's day is found in Chapter IV, of the Memoir by J. E. Austen-Leigh. It has long been divided into three tenements, but apart from a few minor alterations it remains structurally as it was during the Austens' occupation.

It would not be possible to obtain vacant possession of the whole house, nor is it desired ; the present tenants would not, under the society's plan, be in any way disturbed ; but immediate possession would be assured of a large room on the ground floor which (identifiable from its blocked-up window) was the Austens' drawing-room. This would house some very interesting relics which have been promised, and form the nucleus of the place of pilgrimage the society hopes to see established. The society's aim, therefore, is to buy and repair this house, to establish a caretaker, to keep the rest of the premises as living accommodation, but to make certain rooms, particularly associated with Jane Austen, accessible to the public. The owner has agreed to a price of £3,000. Thorough-going repairs

are urgently needed. The society therefore has set itself to raise at least £5,000.

Further information may be had from the hon. secretaries, Jordans, Alton, Hampshire. Subscriptions should be sent to Messrs. Sheen, Stickland and Co., 71, High Street, Alton, Hampshire.

We are yours faithfully,
R. A. AUSTEN-LEIGH, ELIZABETH BOWEN, DAVID CECIL, R. W. CHAPMAN, W. HUGH CURTIS, DOROTHY DARNELL, BEECHER HOGAN, ELIZABETH JENKINS, G. L. KEYNES, MARY LASCELLES, C. S. LEWIS, WILMARTH S. LEWIS, EDWARD MARSH, C. B. TINKER, WELLINGTON, CLOUGH WILLIAMS-ELLIS, MERVYN WINTON.

tours, knowing what to expect and where to find it.

Constance Hill (1844–1929) was a great admirer of Jane Austen, as was her sister Ellen Hill. The two women set out to follow in the footsteps of Jane Austen and her characters, and the result was *Jane Austen: Her Homes and her Friends*, published in 1901. Ellen was an artist, and was able to create 45 line drawings and several water-colour pictures to illustrate the volume. These vary in size and depict Jane Austen's homes, her family, houses she visited, ballrooms she danced in, those famous steps at Lyme, and the churches in which she worshipped. In 1902 an issue of *The Bookman* added 18 photographs of the same places when it reviewed Constance Hill's book. Constance went to some trouble to find members of Jane Austen's family so that she could hear anecdotes and stories, and she was given permission to quote from family manuscripts. Her book went through several editions and was well reviewed,

IMAGE The letter that appeared in *The Times* on December 7, 1946, asking for donations and alerting the public to the need to save the house giving further encouragement and assistance to anyone wanting to see "Jane Austen country".

In 1917, on the centenary of Jane Austen's death, a plaque was unveiled at Chawton Cottage – this plaque (its frame represents a window from Jane's home at 4 Sydney Place, Bath, and is made from oak and bronze) was designed by Ellen Hill and both sisters were responsible for much of the fundraising to pay for it. Visitors could stand outside the cottage and admire the plaque, but were not permitted to go inside. Constance gave talks about Jane Austen after the publication of her book. Their contribution to Jane Austen tourism was a large one.

It would have delighted Constance Hill to know that in 1949 the novelist's house was opened to the public as a museum. Back in 1884 Jane Austen's nephew, Lord Brabourne, felt it necessary to warn any literary pilgrims that Chawton Cottage might not prove worth going to see. "It is built in rather a straggling irregular style", he explained. "There is nothing in it either beautiful or romantic, nothing to associate it with the memory of the immortal Jane." When the memorial plaque financed by Constance Hill was placed on the cottage in 1917, there was no thought of making the square, not especially pretty cottage into a museum. But in 1947 Jane Austen's

great nephew Edward Knight needed to sell off some of the Chawton estate, and once again it was a pair of sisters who got involved. Miss Dorothy Darnell and Miss Beatrix Darnell had founded the Jane Austen Society in 1940. Their society's aim was to purchase the cottage, which was then still inhabited by tenants, and to preserve items that had belonged to Jane or her family. The Darnells wrote to *The Times* asking for donations and alerting the public to the need to save the house. In 1948 the cottage was sold to Thomas Carpenter for £3,000. He restored it and presented it as a gift to the nation, with a newly formed Jane Austen Memorial Trust to run it as a museum. Mr Carpenter's son, Lieutenant Philip Carpenter, had died in battle in 1944, and Philip had loved reading the novels of Jane Austen, so the gift was in his memory and a plaque on the wall of the cottage records this. The house opened as a museum in 1949 and has been one of England's most popular literary homes ever since. Tourists at long last had a proper "shrine" to visit.

So pilgrims to Chawton were now taken care of. They could admire the topaz necklace given to Jane by her brother Charles and immortalised in *Mansfield Park*, the patchwork quilt stitched so industriously by Jane and Cassandra, the first editions, the tiny writing table on which the books were written, and all the other marvellous items on display (including, most recently, the turquoise ring that once belonged to Jane Austen). But what about in Bath? While one could walk the streets in search of places associated with the characters, there was no entry into any of the Bath homes once lived in by Jane Austen. On a wet day, things could be a little dismal for international Janeites who had come to find Jane Austen's Bath. In 1999 a former teacher named David Baldock realised there was a gap in the market and decided to fill it. At 40 Gay Street (Jane Austen lived in Gay Street, but not at No 40) he established the Jane Austen Centre. There visitors can now watch a short film, shop in the gift shop for *Pride and Prejudice* mobile phone covers or Colin Firth key-rings, eat Crawford's crumpets in the Regency tea room, and learn more about Austen's life in Bath from the displays. From this Bath centre has emerged the ten-day Jane Austen Festival that is held in the city each September. Tourists come from around the world to take part in the costumed parade, hear the talks, join in the dances, etc. Bath now offers Jane Austen walking tours, a Jane Austen bus tour, and you can even drink Jane Austen gin in a local gin bar.

It is to be hoped that someone might also feel that there is a gap in the Winchester market. While any visitor can enter the cathedral and pay to stand at Jane Austen's grave, read the nearby information boards or buy a Jane Austen teapot in the gift shop, they can only linger longingly outside the College Street house where the novelist died so young. This house belongs to Winchester College and is lived in by teachers of the school. Some years ago special interest groups were permitted inside, if they made a *very* large donation to the teachers' chosen charity, but that no longer seems to be possible. Today the house is looking slightly neglected. I have been fortunate enough

IMAGES Above, the centenary plaque at Jane Austen's House Museum. Right, "Lizzie" stands guard outside the Jane Austen Centre on Gay Street, Bath

to take a tour group inside this building, which is fascinating architecturally, with parts dating from the Elizabethan era behind its Georgian façade. It was one of the moving experiences of my life to sit in the room where Jane Austen breathed her last, to read to my tour group the wonderful letter written by Cassandra ("I have lost a treasure, such a sister, such a friend as never can have been surpassed. She was the sun of my life, the gilder of every pleasure ...") – an incredibly special moment. I feel sad that others cannot share such magic and hope that Winchester College might soon see the value of jumping on the Jane Austen tourism bandwagon, fixing up the house and opening it to

the public.

When the Laurence Olivier and Greer Garson film of *Pride and Prejudice* was made, Hollywood sets were used for the production. However, as time went on filming techniques changed and real stately homes and gardens began to be used as backdrops. In 1995 the BBC's *Pride and Prejudice* featured a gorgeously dishevelled Colin Firth emerging in a wet white shirt from a pond at Lyme Park, a stately home in Cheshire, and much of the female half of the world went mad. This scene is not, of course, even in the novel, but that didn't seem to matter. Lyme Park had been a quiet National Trust property before this – the odd Sunday stroller enjoyed

the grounds and bought a postcard or two. But Firth's famous swim changed everything. Suddenly Lyme Park was hot tourist property – tourists flocked there in the hopes that Firth/Darcy might just emerge once again from that murky pond. Even if he didn't, they could re-picture that scene in imagination and go home fully satisfied with the experience. Elizabeth Bennet might ask, "What are men to rocks and mountains", but one man and his swim

> Virtual tourism is enormous now. Those unable to travel, can navigate the web to enter the Republic of Pemberley

started a Jane Austen film-tourism industry that flourishes today.

It is lucrative business to have your home connected with a Jane Austen film. Basildon Park (which was Netherfield in the BBC's 1995 *Pride and Prejudice*) enjoyed a 76 per cent increase in visitor numbers after the series was broadcast. Many properties continue to profit from the connection years after filming ended, hosting Jane Austen talks, Jane Austen weekends, offering a "Jane Austen children's trail" through the grounds, selling

postcards of film crews in action in the drawing room. Some places are so eager to join this tourist industry that they will do anything to find a Jane Austen connection, even creating one that never existed. The Rutland Arms, in Derbyshire, advertises itself as the place where Jane Austen stayed while rewriting *Pride and Prejudice*. The accuracy of this claim is highly disputed, yet still tourists visit the pub and feel a thrill at the connection, spurious as it is.

National Trust villages such as Lacock (which was Meryton in the BBC's *Pride and Prejudice* and Highbury in the Gwyneth Paltrow *Emma* movie), a rocky spur in Derbyshire where Keira Knightley stood, wind-swept, and gazed at Pemberley, churches where Austen's heroes and heroine marry, assembly rooms where they dance – all these locations gained increased visitor numbers after featuring in Jane Austen films. And as adaptations show no sign of stopping, the tourism industry will continue to enjoy ardent Janeites hurrying to spend entrance money on sites connected with the movies.

Jane Austen tourism is not limited to places connected with the author's life or novels, or with film versions. Jane Austen is wonderfully transportable. Jane Austen societies now exist in the UK, US, Canada, Australia, New Zealand, Japan, Brazil, the Netherlands, Russia,

Germany, Singapore and Italy. These societies hold conferences, meetings, dances, dinners and special events, which draw tourists from around the world. Literary tours include places connected with Austen – I have taken hundreds of Australians and New Zealanders on an "Exploring the Literary Landscapes of England" tour which features visits to Chawton, Winchester, Lacock and Bath. Jane Austen sites are always a huge drawcard on literary tours.

Virtual tourism is enormous now. Those unable to travel, can navigate the web to enter the Republic of Pemberley. They can admire images of buildings she knew and places where she walked, shopped, ate and wrote. They can travel to a meeting of a book club devoted entirely to the novels of Jane Austen or participate in such book clubs online.

Tourists can go on cruise-ship holidays focusing especially on their favourite novelist, can travel to conferences and festivals, and can enjoy international literary travel via many sites on the web. Jane Austen loved to travel, but had few opportunities. Many of her heroines go on journeys – to Bath, to Derbyshire, to a new home in Devon, to London – and through their travels find happiness in love and marriage. She sent her novels out from Chawton Cottage to make their way – those books have travelled the world

and the brilliance of her writing and the vivid charm of her characters have caused millions, from Lord Tennyson on foot to the modern user of the internet, to seek out the settings of important scenes, to see where the author lived and worked, and to somehow get closer to her characters by following in their footsteps. The Jane Austen tourist industry is alive and well and, like a good quality muslin, shows no signs of fading.

SUSANNAH FULLERTON

Susannah Fullerton is president of the Jane Austen Society of Australia and author of *Jane Austen – Antipodean Views*, *Jane Austen and Crime*, *A Dance with Jane Austen* and *Happily Ever After: Celebrating Jane Austen's Pride and Prejudice*

· · · · ·

IMAGES OF JANE

• • • • •

Who would not wish to own a genuine picture of Jane Austen?
DEIRDRE LE FAYE offers her personal view on the
authentic, the adapted, the imaginary and misattributed

What did Jane Austen look like? As no professional artist ever painted or drew her portrait, we have only descriptions by family and friends, written down later in the 19th century:

Henry, her brother (1771-1850): "...her stature rather exceeded the middle height; her carriage and deportment were quiet, but graceful; her features were separately good; their assemblage produced an unrivalled expression of that cheerfulness, sensibility, and benevolence, which were her real characteristics; her complexion was of the finest texture – it might with truth be said, that her eloquent blood spoke through her modest cheek ..."

Anna, her niece (1793-1872): "The Figure tall & slight, but not drooping, well balanced, as was proved by her quick firm step – Her complexion of that rather rare sort which seems the peculiar property of light brunettes – A mottled skin, not fair, but perfectly clear & healthy in hue; the fine naturally curling hair, neither light nor dark; the bright hazel eyes to match, & the rather small but well-shaped nose."

Caroline, her niece (1805-80): "Her face was rather round than long – she had a bright, but not a pink colour – a clear brown complexion and very good hazle [sic] eyes ... Her hair, a darkish brown, curled naturally – it was in short curls round her face She always wore a cap – Such was the custom with ladies who were not quite young ..."

James Edward, her nephew (1798-1874): "In complexion she was a clear brunette with a rich colour; she had full round cheeks, with mouth and nose small and well formed, light hazel eyes and brown hair forming natural curls close round her face.'"

Sir Egerton Brydges, her friend and an acquaintance of the family (1762-1837): "She was fair and handsome, slight and elegant, but with cheeks a little too full."

Hilary Davidson, the dress historian, recently studied and replicated a brown-and-gold silk pelisse reputed to have belonged to Jane Austen – perhaps the one she mentions in her letter No 105, August 23-24, 1814 – and this study has shown that Jane was between 5ft 6in and 5ft 8in (167-173cm) in height, with bust, waist and hips measuring respectively 30in, 24in and 30in – slight indeed.

The only authentic portrait is Cassandra's pencil and watercolour half-length sketch, about 4in by 3in, made probably c1810, which is now in the National Portrait Gallery in London. It shows Jane seated on a simple wooden chair, looking to the left and arms folded; she wears a small, frilly-edged mob-cap, from beneath which a few curls escape on to her forehead, and a very plain short-sleeved dress, its low-cut bodice filled in up to the neck with a muslin tucker. Only the face is tinted, showing that she had hazel eyes, dark brows and hair, and pink cheeks, and

IMAGE The only authentic portrait of Jane Austen, by her sister Cassandra

had inherited her father's straight nose, rather thin-lipped mouth and heavy jaw-line.

Cassandra also painted a back view, about 7.5in x 5in, of her sister dressed in blue and "sitting down out of doors on a hot day, with her bonnet strings untied", as Anna later described it. Just a hint of a pink cheek is shown, but the dangling bonnet strings hide Jane's profile. This is dated 1804 and must have been done during the

IMAGES Left, a silhouette, entitled *L'aimable Jane*, which was discovered in 1944. Above, Cassandra also painted a back view of her sister in 1804

posthumous portrait of Jane was made when James Edward Austen-Leigh started to write *A Memoir of Jane Austen* in 1869. Cassandra's sketch had descended to Admiral Charles Austen's eldest daughter, Cassy-Esten (1808-97), and she lent it to her cousin so that a more polished version could be made that would be suitable for publication. Austen-Leigh, who was then the vicar of Bray in Berkshire, called in a local artist, James Andrews (1801-76) of Maidenhead, to copy and "improve" the sketch. This was done under the superintendence of Austen-Leigh and his sisters Anna and Caroline, and when completed they considered the likeness sufficiently good to justify offering it to the public as a portrait of Jane Austen. Andrews produced a watercolour miniature on card, size about 5.5in x 4in; he altered the chair on which Jane sits, making it more elegant – dining-room rather than kitchen – and put more colour into his version, showing a blue ribbon in the cap and a blue waistband to the dress. It is not known whether these touches of blue were his own idea, or whether Austen-Leigh and his sisters could recall that Jane had indeed worn a dress with such trimmings and requested him to make the additions. This miniature descended to Austen-Leigh's youngest children, Mary-Augusta (1838-1922) and William (1843-1921), and from them

family's summer holiday in the West Country that year; it remains in family ownership.

The National Portrait Gallery also owns a silhouette, entitled *L'aimable Jane*, which was discovered in 1944 tipped into the second volume of a copy of *Mansfield Park* (1816 edition). Unfortunately there is no provenance for the book, but as Dr Chapman said at the time of its discovery: "Who would insert, in a copy of *Mansfield Park*, a portrait of any other Jane than its author?"

The first attempt to create a

IMAGES A steel-engraved image of Jane Austen, which will also appear on the Bank of England's £10 note, right

passed down the Austen-Leigh family until sold at Sotheby's on December 10, 2013.

A steel-engraved version of the Andrews miniature was made by the Lizars family, an Edinburgh firm of engravers, and was used as frontispiece to Austen-Leigh's *Memoir* when it was published in 1870; this is now the best-known image of Jane, having been reproduced many times since then. It will appear on the Bank of England's new £10 note in 2017.

When the *Memoir* appeared, Jane's nieces were lukewarm about this engraving. Cassy-Esten wrote: "I think the portrait is very much superior to any thing that could have been expected from the sketch it was taken from. – It is a very pleasing, sweet face, – tho', I confess, to not thinking it much like the original – but that, the public will not be able to detect." Caroline's views were similar: "The portrait is better than I expected – as considering its early date, and that it has lately passed through the hands of painter and engraver – I did not reckon upon finding any likeness – but there is a look which I recognise as hers – and though the general resemblance is not strong, yet as it represents a pleasant countenance it is so far a truth –." Later on she agreed with a comment from Edward Knight's daughter Lizzy Rice (1800-84), about the eyes: "they are larger than the truth: that is, rounder, & more open." A friend from the Chawton days thought: "Jane's likeness is hardly what I remember there is a look, & that is all – I remember her as a tall thin spare person, with very high cheekbones great colour – sparkling Eyes not large but joyous and intelligent. The face by no means so broad & plump as represented; perhaps it was taken when very young, but the Cap looks womanly."

After the publication of the *Memoir*, other artists, professional and amateur, started to copy the frontispiece and adapt it to their own tastes, from 1870 right up to the present day. Practically every biography or new edition of Jane's novels uses a form of the engraving on the cover or as an illustration; it would be impossible to keep track of all these versions, some of which approach caricature, so only those which are unusual or which have been the subject of recent publicity will be mentioned here.

1. Watercolour, half-length, 12in x 9.5in. This portrays a blandly pretty, pale-faced young woman in a white dress, sitting in an arm-chair, but no other background is given. It is a coloured version of the *Memoir* engraving by an unskilled amateur – the face is flat and wide and the body fat and clumsy. Much more dark hair is shown beneath the cap, the blue ribbons are more in evidence, the gathered muslin neckline has been changed into a string of coral beads, and a brown shawl is draped round her elbows. The sitter's right forearm is hidden by this shawl, but the left hand is a podgy paw resting on the wooden arm of the chair.

This picture surfaced in 1945, when it was owned by an elderly lady, Miss Margaret Stevenson, who believed that it represented Jane Austen. Dr Chapman took it to the National Portrait Gallery, but both he and they dismissed it as not being genuine. It was sold at Sotheby's on November 27, 1945, and

Bank of England

Ten Pounds

"I declare after all there is no enjoyment like reading!"

Jane Austen

bought by a Mr Robert Tritton. In 1936 Mr Tritton and his wife had purchased the near-derelict Godmersham Park, restored the house and refurnished it in 18th-century style. The then vicar of Godmersham, the Rev S. G. Brade-Birks, later called on Miss Stevenson in the hope of finding out more about her picture. However, all she could remember was that circa 1887-88 it was already hanging in her mother's room in their house in Dover. Mrs Stevenson was not interested in Jane Austen and thought poorly of the picture, relegating it to the box-room; the house was bombed in 1916 but the picture survived. The National Portrait Gallery inspected it again in 1959, but no watermark, signature or date was found.

The picture remained at Godmersham until Mrs Tritton died and the house contents were sold at Christie's on June 6-9, 1983. In 2000 the present owner thought it might represent Cassandra Austen rather than Jane, and lent it to the Jane Austen Memorial Trust for display at Chawton Cottage on this basis. However, lacking in provenance as it is, the picture can have no claim to be a genuine representation of either Jane

"Returning to her seat to finish a note." Chap XXX.

IMAGES Left, in this picture Jane Austen appears to be wearing a wedding ring. Above, HM Brock's drawing for *Mansfield Park* inspired one of the imagined portraits of Jane Austen

or Cassandra. It was presumably created at some time post-1870 and given to Mrs Stevenson before the mid-1880s.

2. Another steel engraving, a much elaborated version of that in the *Memoir*. It shows Jane three-quarter length, sitting in a chair draped in fabric and with swagged curtains behind her; a low table to the right bears several books together with an inkwell and quill. She is holding a book or portfolio on her knee, and her left hand, which rests on this, displays a wedding ring – hence this picture is sometimes referred

to as the Wedding-Ring Portrait. The artist had evidently not been informed that Jane never married. The original of this engraving is an oil painting, 14in x 10in, executed in black and white specifically for re-working as an engraving. It was presumably created for Evert A. Duyckinck, as it appears in his *Portrait Gallery of Eminent Men and Women of Europe and America* (New York 1873). The original oil painting was purchased by an American lady in the second half of the last century, who found it in a flea market in Columbus, New Jersey.

There are a number of imagined portraits, including:

1. Unknown artist, post-1898. This picture was Lot 1130 of the Godmersham sale in 1983, when it was catalogued as: "English School, circa 1810: Portrait of Jane Austen, full length, in white dress, seated writing at a table / pencil and watercolour 11½ by 7½ inches." However, it is very clearly a modern mock-up: a miniaturised version of the *Memoir* face has been awkwardly dabbed on to a body and background, which is composed partly from a Hugh Thomson illustration showing Elizabeth Bennet sitting at a writing table (the frontispiece to the George Allen edition of *Pride and Prejudice*, London 1894), and partly from a H.M. Brock illustration of Fanny Price at her writing table (the frontispiece to

vol. II of the Dent edition of *Mansfield Park*, London 1898) – and must therefore be dated 1898 at the very earliest.

2. Violet Helm, 1909. The frontispiece, in black and white, for William Henry Helm's *Jane Austen and her Country-House Comedy* (London, 1909). It is a half-length of a pensive curly-haired young woman sitting at a table, quill in hand and large sheets of paper before her. The size and present ownership (if it survives) are unknown.

3. Percy Fitzgerald, 1912. Fitzgerald (1834-1925) was an author and amateur sculptor who wrote a number of lightweight biographies of 18th-century personalities. He created a bust, in bronze or perhaps bronze-coloured plaster, and used it as frontispiece to his short biography *Jane Austen, A Criticism and Appreciation* (London, 1912), without acknowledging that it was completely imaginary. He persuaded Bath city council to place this bust in the Pump Room, but after complaints by William and Mary-Augusta Austen-Leigh, who pointed out to the Mayor of Bath that it bore no resemblance to Jane Austen, it was removed from display. Its present location (if it survives) is unknown.

4. Alexander Strahan Buchanan, c 1914. Watercolour on cardboard, about 10in x 7in. A rather worn handwritten inscription on the reverse reads: "An attempt to realize a truer idea of Jane Austen by Alex S. Buchanan – From the

sketch by Cassandra & Descriptions [possibly some words rubbed away here] & Known characteristics." It is an enlarged and brightened version of the Andrews miniature, extended into a half-length, and shows Jane standing at a table, her hands resting on three small books, set against a full background of a Georgian domestic interior. Buchanan was a figure painter, who exhibited at the Royal Academy from 1902 to 1914. He was presumably inspired to create his portrait after the publication of *Jane Austen, her Life and Letters*, by William and R. A. Austen-Leigh in 1913, and evidently was allowed to see the Andrews miniature for this purpose. The picture was sold at Mallams in Oxford in 2006, without provenance, and was purchased by the present writer.

5. Melissa Dring, 2002. This half-length study in pastel, size 21"x 26", showing Jane sitting in front of her writing-slope and looking to the left, was commissioned by the Jane Austen Centre, with the aim of representing Austen during her years of Bath residence. The artist stated: "I wanted to bring out something of Jane's lively and humorous character, so evident in her novels and all contemporary accounts of her. Cassandra's drawing may have been quite like Jane physically, but has failed to catch her sparkle." Dring studied the known portraits of other members of the Austen family; she

IMAGES Top, Melissa Dring's 2002 study for the Jane Austen Centre, Bath. Above, an image from c1818 that some believe could be of Jane Austen

also took very literally Austen-Leigh's statement in the *Memoir* that Jane had "a rich colour", for when the picture was published there were comments to the effect that she looked as if she were suffering from sunburn. In 2014, Dring also created a life-size waxwork for the centre that was supposedly a likeness of Jane Austen.

6. Unknown artist, ?1818. This portrait could be classed as either imaginary or misattributed. It is half-length, plumbago on vellum, about 6in x 5in, badly drawn by an unskilled amateur. The subject is a lavishly dressed and bejewelled middle-aged lady, with large nose and pale eyes, apparently sitting at a small round table upon which is a curled-up sleeping cat, and writing from right to left on a sheaf of loose paper (a physical impossibility), with eyes upraised as if seeking inspiration from the heavens. The background shows the commonplace arrangement of swagged curtain and classical column on the left, with the west front of Westminster Abbey seen through an imaginary window on the right. On the back is a small black-ink inscription in a scholarly Edwardian handwriting "Miss Jane Austin" [sic]. Its first known owner was Sir John Foster (1903-82), a bachelor lawyer and MP; he instructed his executrix to destroy all his personal papers, so the provenance of the drawing is lost forever. In 1982 it was

bought by a dealer, and from him passed to Mr Roy Davids, who in turn sold it at Bonhams in March 2011, when it was bought by Dr Paula Byrne, the present owner, who used it in her biography of Jane Austen published in 2013.

If this is to be considered as an imaginary portrait, then it can be assumed that the artist, whoever s/he may have been, had read Henry Austen's "Biographical Notice" of his sister, published in 1818, and invented this image accordingly. The elements of the portrait are symbolic – the lady's closely-fitting lace-trimmed mob-cap looks at first sight like a laurel wreath awarded for literary achievement; her elaborate high-necked long-sleeved dress, fashionable c1815, suggests rich respectability; and her various rings and necklaces demonstrate likewise that she was well off, not a poor hack writer starving in a garret. The sleeping cat on the table beside her suggests spinsterhood – a pet instead of a child – and the view of Westminster Abbey could confirm Henry's statement that "She was thoroughly religious and devout." None of these symbols, however, relates in any way to Jane's life. Likely misattributions:

1. The Byrne Portrait (as it is now

IMAGE The life-size waxwork that was created by Melissa Dring for the Jane Austen Centre in Bath in 2014

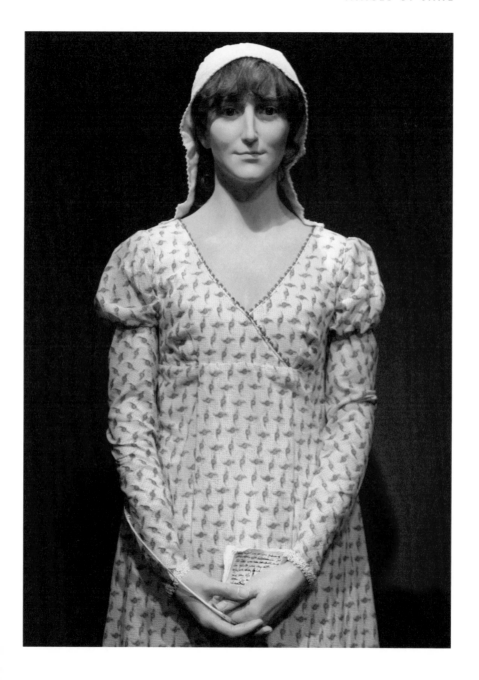

family own a full-length portrait in oils, showing a young girl in a white dress, which they believe depicts Jane Austen aged about twelve – therefore meaning it was painted about 1787. However, art historians and experienced dress historians have said that the painting cannot predate 1800. In 1996 I identified the sitter as a Kentish relation, Mary Anne Campion (1797-1825), daughter of Jane's second cousin, namesake, and almost exact contemporary, Jane Austen of Kippington (1776-1857), and suggested that it was painted about 1806. The latest research by the National Portrait Gallery has confirmed that the canvas upon which the portrait was painted was sold at some date between 1801 and 1806.

3. James Stanier Clarke's drawing. In 1994 the late R. J. Wheeler publicised his ownership of the "Friendship Album" compiled by the Rev James

being called). If this is to be considered as a genuine portrait, then the sitter was probably in the family of one of the Abbey's resident clerics. She evidently wished to be portrayed as a wealthy and high-minded lady, and her literary interests may have been the composition of religious tracts or verses.

2. The Rice Portrait. The Rice

IMAGE The Rice Portrait. The author believes the sitter in this portrait to have been a Kentish relation of Jane Austen

Stainer Clarke, the Prince Regent's librarian, who met Jane Austen when she visited Carlton House on November 13, 1815. Wheeler theorised that Clarke was so impressed by Jane that he painted her portrait from memory and stuck it into his album. However, dated entries in the collection show that it was compiled between 1791 and 1804 and this portrait – a full-length watercolour, about 6in high – shows a plump young lady smartly dressed in the fashions of spring 1797, which were quite different from those of 1815. The sitter was probably Stanier Clarke's sister.

4. Winchester Cathedral owns a silhouette, size about 3in x 1½in, painted upon card, which is inscribed on the reverse: Jane Austin, [sic] done by herself in 1815. However, this inscription is in modern handwriting and blue-black ink, and the fashion of the silhouette itself shows it was created very much later in the 19th century – perhaps 1895. It probably shows Admiral Charles Austen's granddaughter Jane (1849-1928).

SOURCES

James-Edward Austen-Leigh: *A Memoir of Jane Austen, and other family recollections*; ed. Kathryn Sutherland (OUP World's Classics, 2002).

Mary Augusta Austen-Leigh: *James Echvard Austen Leigh, a memoir by his daughter* (1911).

Hilary Davidson: 'Reconstructing Jane Austen's Silk Pelisse, 1812-1814', in *Costume*, 49/2 (2015), 198-223.

Deirdre Le Faye: *Jane Austen, A Family Record*; CUP (2nd edn, 2004). *Jane Austen's Letters* (ed); OUP (4th edn, 2011). 'A Literary Portrait Re-examined – Jane Austen and Mary Anne Campion'; in *The Book Collector* 45/4, Winter 1996, 508-25. 'Imaginary Portraits of Jane Austen'; in The Jane Austen Society's Report for 2007 (Winchester 2008), 42-52. This article discusses several other modern portraits not mentioned here. 'Three telltale words; or, not Jane Austen's portrait"; in *The Times Literary Supplement*, May 4, 2012, 14-15.

Richard Walker: *Regency Portraits*; National Portrait Gallery, London (1985).

DEIRDRE LE FAYE

· · · · ·

CAPTURING LIFE, NOT DEATH

. . . . .

Stories of lives both distinguished and dissolute were recorded in the regency press. **NIGEL STARCK** explores the obituary pages of the time – and finds that Jane herself was shabbily treated

"**T**he Princess is dead!" cried *The Evening Star*. For column after column, it then launched into a lavish obituary, lamenting the loss of "the hope and admiration of an affectionate people". This was November 1817. In sentiments that would be echoed on losing another princess 180 years later, the British press wept with its readers at the death of Princess Charlotte, only child of the Prince Regent and Caroline of Brunswick. She had died at the age of 21 in giving birth to a stillborn son. Here, as is so often the case in a quest for the spirit of times past, it is the newspaper obituaries that are notably revealing. When written well, they offer an assured portrait of what it was like to live – and to die – in the Regency age. Poor Charlotte's account depicts the mood of public mourning: all theatres and other places of entertainment would be closed until after her burial, and the drawing of the national lottery was postponed indefinitely. Britain had lost, in one grossly mismanaged episode of childbirth, the most popular member of its royal family and her son, each a prospective Hanoverian monarch.

At the age of 16, Charlotte had read *Sense and Sensibility*, confiding in a letter (and displaying some rather shaky spelling and grammar): "Maryanne & me are very alike in disposition ... the same imprudence."

Jane Austen discovered soon afterwards that the Prince Regent was another admirer of her novels. Her brother Henry had been taken ill, and doctors were summoned. One of them happened to have court connections. When he found that she was in London tending to Henry, arrangements were made for her to visit Carlton House, the Prince's London home, where Jane met James Stanier Clarke, the resident librarian. These events imposed on her an obligation to dedicate *Emma* to the Prince Regent on its publication in 1815.

Privately she had expressed a profound dislike of the Prince – in common with popular sentiment subsequently let loose in a violent obituary published by *The Times* at his death in 1830. It attacked his "most reckless, unceasing and unbounded prodigality", accusing him of being "initiated in all the vices" in his youth, as a consequence of which he pursued a way of life "little higher than that of animal indulgence". In sum, it supplies an early example of explicit character assessment – or, in this instance, assassination – by the power

IMAGE The funeral procession of Princess Charlotte in 1817

of obituary. Fawning and pretence could be set aside; the dead cannot sue for defamation.

Twelve years earlier the *Evening Mail* had blamed Queen Charlotte, the Prince's mother, for his shortcomings. Thrusting a similar posthumous poniard into public remembrance of the late Queen, the *Mail* obituary column of November 18, 1818, suggested that she had failed miserably as a parent:

How far the late Queen of England acquitted of the sacred obligations of a mother towards her offspring, from their infancy upwards ... we, in common with the public, are perhaps not quite accurately informed. Were it safe to found a judgment on the recent dispersion of the Princes of the Blood Royal, and of some of the Princesses, we might, however reluctantly, conclude that Her Majesty had not altogether

succeeded in attaching to her the hearts of her children.

This obituary then had a dig at her appearance, while acknowledging that the King himself was not dissatisfied with his consort:

Her Majesty's figure was very pleasing, but her countenance, though not without attraction when she smiled, could not boast any claim to beauty. It was, however, a well-known fact that the King declared himself satisfied with his connubial fortune.

The *Evening Mail* did note also, though, that the Queen had brought some sense of Germanic order to the royal household's financial management. She was constantly "attentive to the payments of her own tradesmen ... when the King's civil list was disgracefully in arrears".

This pursuit of obituary by character study, rather than slavish engagement with formal curriculum vitae, was pioneered by *The Gentleman's Magazine*, a monthly miscellany that reached its editorial zenith during

IMAGE Left, the Prince Regent. Below, the Prince of Orange kneels before Princess Charlotte

Jane Austen's lifetime. It avoided the moral high ground, appraising lives that had undermined society as well as those that had adorned it. Peter Defaile, said to have been the "most notorious villain as ever became the scourge of private life", duly appeared on the obituary pages of *The Gentleman's Magazine* of January 1783. He had been the second son "of a good family" in the west of England, he qualified as an attorney and then forged a will so that his elder brother was disinherited. After spending the spoils, of more than £40,000, in a prolonged chapter of dissipation, Defaile became a singularly effective, if sinister, 18th-century rake:

> He insinuated himself, as soon as he found poverty approaching, into the good graces of a beautiful young lady of great fortune, whom he married, and spent all her money; and in succession, in the space of eleven or twelve years, married five more wives, all fortunes [sic], all which money he also spent, and these ladies died so very opportunely to make way for their successors, that when Defaile's character was better known nobody made any doubt of his having poisoned them.

The obituary then traces a history of gambling, arson and insurance fraud, the swindling "of an old lady out of a great deal of money" and the killing of an opponent in a duel. Eventually, overtaken by "gout and stone", he died in a debtors' prison in Flanders.

Two months later *The Gentleman's Magazine* published the salutary tale of a prominent entertainer fallen on hard times. Thomas Lowe had been a star of Sadler's Wells and Vauxhall Gardens, regularly earning £1,000 a year. Yet, it continued, he had "constantly dissipated the whole of it" and was rendered in his declining years "an object of charity as well as pity". There were *Gentleman's Magazine* obituaries too of James Heaton, "one of the most formidable poachers in

---

184   *Obituary; with Anecdotes of remarkable Persons.*   [Aug.

July 18.

At Winchester, Miss Jane Austen, youngest daughter of Rev. George Austen, Rector of Steventon, Hants, authoress of " Emma," " Mansfield Park," " Pride and Prejudice," and " Sense and Sensibility."

the kingdom"; of Winifred Griffith, a baronet's daughter who died "in distressed circumstances" following "an imprudent marriage" and "the villainy of an attorney"; and of the "Reverend Mr Withers" in Newgate prison. The unfortunate clergyman had been gaoled "for a libel on Mrs Fitzherbert" (whom the Prince Regent had secretly married in defiance of the Royal Marriages Act). The obituary attributes his death to "too violent an effort at a game of fives", which "threw him into a great perspiration". He had then "imprudently sat without his coat and waistcoat during a shower of rain", developed "a putrid fever" and expired.

However, *The Gentleman's Magazine* could manage only a closeted exercise in obituary rendition at the death of Jane Austen herself. Its inadequate paragraph served as an indicator of the erratic journalism that prevailed at the time: the same edition devoted three pages to an obituary of Madame de Staël, the writer who had dismissed the Austen *oeuvre* as *vulgaire*.

As David Gilson has recounted, in a chapter of *The Jane Austen Handbook* (The Athlone Press, 1986), there were 11 newspaper and periodical notices acknowledging Jane's death

IMAGE The inadequate obituary of Jane Austen that appeared in *The Gentleman's Magazine* in August 1817

in 1817, four months before that of Princess Charlotte. In *The Gentleman's Magazine*, rather than the full-blooded recognition that she deserved, there was simply this: "At Winchester, Miss Jane Austen, youngest daughter of Rev. George Austen, Rector of Steventon, Hants, authoress of 'Emma', 'Mansfield Park', 'Pride and Prejudice', and 'Sense and Sensibility'." (Those were the four novels published at that juncture.)

The newspaper accounts were little better. Some employed a similarly cryptic summary; others a vapid engagement with eulogy. It would seem that this collective understatement had been nurtured by her early habits of anonymity, the family's innate wariness and her relatives' talent for destroying correspondence. Yet this was the woman who, in a surviving letter to her sister, declared: "If I am a wild beast, I cannot help it. It is not my own fault." The failure to secure public acknowledgment through the obituary columns was, rather, the fault of those who sought to restrain Jane Austen's natural inclination for creative wilfulness.

It is known from the early books that she preferred anonymity, not necessarily because of shyness but perhaps because she considered it *arriviste* or *gauche* to seek self-publicity. There was no contemporary biography either. Consequently, the Austen name would for decades remain obscure. In *Jane's Fame: How Jane Austen Conquered the World* (Canongate 2009), Claire Harman says that "'by the 1860s when the first tourists sought out the writer's grave in Winchester Cathedral, the verger had no idea what she was famous for". This seems quite extraordinary today, such is the global pilgrimage by 'Janeites' to sacred sites associated with their literary heroine.

> The Gentleman's Magazine could manage only a closeted excercise in obituary rendition at the death of Jane Austen

That later mistress of feminist letters, Charlotte Brontë, had achieved a much more enlightening memorial in print at her death in 1855. Harriet Martineau, writing for *The Daily News* (a paper founded by Charles Dickens), supplied an intimate portrait:

> *The account of the school in Jane Eyre is only too true.... She was the smallest of women, and it was that school which stunted her growth ... [and] being short-sighted to excess, she wrote in little square paper books, held close to her eyes, and [the first copy] in pencil. On she went, writing incessantly for three weeks; by which time she had carried her heroine away from Thornfield, and was herself in a fever.*

By this stage of its development the obituary had become an important instrument in the cause of recording history. The Regency and the Victorian newspapers were practising a polished version of an art that goes back to the very beginnings of the popular press. Early instances can be found in the newspapers that emerged under the rule of Charles II, who appointed Roger L'Estrange as both court journalist and official censor. L'Estrange had been a serving Cavalier in England's civil war, raised a regiment in Norfolk for Charles I, was captured by the Roundheads, tried at court-martial and sentenced to death. He escaped from prison, fled to the Continent, appearing again at the return of the monarchy to ingratiate himself with Charles II.

As the king's censor, from 1662 to 1679, he hounded printers suspected of seditious practice; one victim, John Twyn, who had printed pamphlets seen as inciting civil unrest, was hanged and disembowelled. After that, L'Estrange was untroubled. He concentrated on his own publishing licence, awarded by royal decree, starting in 1663 with *The Intelligencer* (on Mondays) and *The*

Newes (on Thursdays). He also makes a firm claim to being recognised as the first obituary editor. His newspapers, when scrutinised under today's journalistic microscope, demonstrate a capacity for instant biography – the true test of what is, and what it not, a genuine obituary. According to the *Routledge Encyclopedia of Narrative Theory* (Routledge 2005):

> *The obituary offers an appraisal of a life in the form of a brief biography – published in a newspaper, magazine or journal. It is important to note the appraisal factor, for it is this element which distinguishes an obituary from a standard news story about death. While the intent of the latter is to supply an account of a deceased person's life, often with information also on the circumstances of death, the obituary provides an assessment of its subject's character, achievements, and effect on society.*

Such character assessment is apparent in his ornate, but historically significant, obituary of a dead royalist in a May 1664 issue of *The Newes*:

> *This week affords but little but the sad news of the death of that great Minister of State, William, Earle of Glencairn, Lord High Chancellour of Scotland, a Person most Eminent, and well known in all his Majestyes Dominions, both for the Gallantry of his Spirit in the Noble Attempts against the Usurpers, as also for his sufferings during those times of Usurpation, and the many signal Services he hath performed in that high Station, wherein his Majesty most deservedly placed him since his happy Restauration. He dyed the 30th of the Instant of a Feavour in the 49th year of his Age, Beloved of his Prince, and Bewayled of all Ranks of his Majestyes Subjects.*

This concern for character appraisal had gained a more assured, less flowery, voice by the following century. It attained, too, a significant measure of international adoption. Benjamin Franklin, apprenticed as a printer to his brother James and later to become a scientist and statesman of international repute, took this unencumbered style of journalism with him when he moved to Philadelphia. There, when still in his early twenties, he bought in 1729 a struggling newspaper with an ungainly title, *The Universal Instructor in all Arts and Sciences and Pennsylvania Gazette*.

Franklin immediately ditched all but the last two words, won – by the superior quality of his work – the government printing contract which had previously been held by Andrew Bradford (of *The American Weekly Mercury*), and ran this enterprise so

which was stationed in the colonies at that time. Franklin's *Weekly Mercury* told its readers:

> She had been a great traveller, was in the Army with her Husband in Flanders, Germany, Spain and Italy, was at the taking of Port Royal, and in all the Wars in Ireland, had been at the taking of several Prizes, receiv'd a Wound in her Leg in Flanders; she was Woman of undaunted Courage and Resolution to the very last ... and according to her desire, was carried to her Grave with the King's Jack [a flag], a Sword and Scabbard across her Pall.

Another virtue of this *Mercury* obituary is that its subject was indeed dead; the newspaper's account achieved validity accordingly. Such had not been the case in 1816, when the poet Samuel Taylor Coleridge found himself the prematurely "killed off" by a British newspaper. Sitting in the coffee room of a hotel, he heard his name declaimed by a man reading aloud a newspaper's inquest report. Coleridge immediately demanded to see the paper, which was handed to him with the remark: "It was very extraordinary that Coleridge the poet should have hanged himself just after the success of his play; but he was always a strange mad fellow." Summoning up his oratory, Coleridge replied: "Indeed, sir, it is a

successfully that by 1749 he was able to devote his energies to science and politics instead. Along the way he delivered to American readers an obituary style relieved of piety and naive eulogy. In 1734, his newspaper marked the death of an adventurous woman with a lively obituary: Elizabeth Pothecary, 68, wife of the master of arms serving on HMS *Scarborough*,

IMAGE Jeremy Bentham's auto-icon remains on public display in London

most extraordinary thing that he should have hanged himself, be the subject of an inquest, and yet that he should at this moment be speaking to you." The inquest was apparently told that "a gentleman in black" had been cut down from a tree in Hyde Park, without papers in his clothing. The only identifying mark was the name 'S. T. Coleridge' on the shirt he was wearing.

The art of obituary composition is to capture accurately and persuasively in print an impression of life rather than death. That was not quite enough for the British philosopher Jeremy Bentham. In its 1832 obituary of Bentham, *The Times* explained that its subject insisted on a physical presence too:

> It was a part of the will of the late Mr Bentham that his body should be devoted to the purpose of improving the science of anatomy ... He looked calm and serene, presenting, as Dr Southwood Smith observed, an appearance that might reconcile those who have the most horror ... [of] the aspect of death.

After that dissection, Bentham's head was preserved, his skeleton clothed, and the assembled auto-icon (as he called it) placed on display at University College London. Today, the auto-icon remains on public display, although the head is a wax replica. The original preservation process failed, leaving the flesh darkened and disfigured. The preserved head is now held in the college vaults.

As for his obituary, as for all revelatory obituaries, its paragraphs help to scale the barriers of time travel. This instant exercise in biography, above other forms of newspaper journalism, has the power to deliver an account of what it was like to be a citizen of communities past. Today it can, with safety, be considered as a prime instrument of history. It remains a disservice to the obituary art – and to Austen aficionados everywhere – that Jane and her royal reader Charlotte were accorded such dramatic contrasts in column inches.

NIGEL STARCK

Nigel Starck is Assistant Editor of *Jane Austen's Regency World* magazine and author of *Life After Death: the Art of the Obituary*

• • • • •

LUST AND ATTRACTION

· · · · ·

We may think that Jane Austen's writing is all sweet and demure, but there's plenty of lust and attraction to be found both between her pages and in her life, writes **PENELOPE FRIDAY**

Why did Mr and Mrs Bennet marry? Why is the most off-colour joke in Jane Austen made in the novel with the most prudish heroine? Why does Marianne fall so hard and fast for Willoughby? And why oh why does, despite this, Jane Austen have a reputation for writing polite, "genteel" novels?

Sex and sexuality are at the heart of Jane Austen's novels. How could they not be, when the "happy ever after" that her books espouse is marriage? Unless we are expected to believe that Elizabeth and Darcy (for example) were going into a purely platonic relationship, the idea of sexual attraction must be considered as an important part of their love affair. And with sexy ne'er-do-wells such

as Willoughby, Wickham and Henry Crawford littering Austen's novels, as well as subtle insinuations of other types of relationship (it is difficult to believe that Mary Crawford's comment in *Mansfield Park,* when she comments that "Of *Rears* and *Vices* I saw enough" was not meant to reference homosexual sex, for example), it is impossible to consider Jane Austen's novels without thinking about the role of lust and attraction in them.

There's no two ways about it: Jane Austen knew all about sex appeal and sexual attraction. But where did Jane Austen get her knowledge of lust and attraction from, given that she herself never married? Of course, an actual marriage does not need to take place for someone to be aware of sex and attractiveness; and it is clear when looking at Jane Austen's letters and life that she certainly had some personal experience in the area. At 20 she had, at least, a brief flirtation with a gentleman of the name of Tom Lefroy and, at most, fell in love with him; it is difficult to tell

IMAGE Tom Lefroy in later life. Jane Austen enjoyed a brief flirtation with him when she was 20

the depth of her feelings from the little one gleans from her letters to Cassandra at the time. Certainly, she wrote of a meeting at a ball with him:

> "I am almost afraid to tell you how my Irish friend and I behaved. Imagine to yourself everything most profligate and shocking in the way of dancing and sitting down together."

She also acknowledges that he has been

teased for their closeness. Despite the implication in the recent film *Becoming Jane* that Tom Lefroy was the great romance in Jane Austen's life, it is in fact suggested by Deirdre Le Faye that:

> *It is highly unlikely that Tom proposed or that Jane ever really believed he would do so. However, Mr and Mrs Lefroy had seen enough of their mutual attraction to take fright at the idea of an engagement between so youthful and penniless a pair, and Tom was sent off rapidly to London.*

Tom was the nephew of a great friend of Jane's – Anne Lefroy – and perhaps the most telling comment about their attraction comes in a much later letter from Jane Austen to her sister. When Tom stayed again with his aunt nearly three years later, Jane and he did not meet. When Anne visits Jane after he has left, Jane tells Cassandra that "she did not once mention the name of the former to me, and I was too proud to make any inquiries". Being too proud to make inquiries after a gentleman one had known several years earlier suggests at least some sort of lingering feeling for him.

There are also less proven stories of other love interests in Jane Austen's life. In 1801 her family went to Sidmouth for the summer, where it is said that Jane fell deeply and mutually in love with an unknown gentleman. Sadly, the gentleman's brother wrote to inform her family that the man had died. There are no letters from Jane for months after this time – either Cassandra destroyed them or Jane was too distressed to write; so details are scanty about the state of Jane's feelings.

A more salacious version of the above story comes from Andrew Norman, who wrote the book *Jane Austen: An Unrequited Love*. He suggests that the gentleman in question was a clergyman of the name of Samuel Bicknall, whom Jane Austen already knew. He also claims that the letter announcing the man's death was a forgery – written by Jane's sister Cassandra, who was in love with Bicknall herself and jealous of the relationship. This, Norman says, explains the lack of letters: either Jane was too hurt by Cassandra to write to her, or the letters would have exposed Cassandra's treachery and were thus destroyed.

Certain it is that Jane Austen rejected the one proposal she is known to have received, because she did not feel the right emotion towards Harris Bigg-Wither to marry him. She would later write to her niece (apropos the niece's own love affair): "Anything is to be preferred and endured rather than marrying without affection."

So it is important to remember that while Jane Austen might never have married, this does not mean that she had no personal experience of lust and sexual attraction. And, as with so many things, in her writing she draws more out of it than most of the rest of us would manage, no matter our level of sexual experience. So what makes someone sexually attractive, in Jane Austen's eyes?

It's not just a case of beauty. Jane Bennet in *Pride and Prejudice* is beautiful, yet Elizabeth has a far stronger pull of attraction to men. Although Jane attracts the attention of Charles Bingley, and it seems that she has had poetry written about her in the past, it is Elizabeth who in *Pride and Prejudice* has an embarrassment of suitors. Even leaving Mr Collins out of the equation (for he, we are told, fixed originally on Jane for the simple reason that she was the oldest), Elizabeth is demonstrated to attract Wickham, who treats her with amazing attention considering her lack of fortune;

Colonel Fitzwilliam, for whom her lack of fortune again is the stumbling block to any marriage; and Darcy who, despite Elizabeth's disastrous relations and inferior situation in life, invites

IMAGE Adrian Lukis as Mr Wickham in *Pride and Prejudice* (1995)

her to marry him not once, but twice. Given the extremely small number of appropriately aged gentleman in *Pride and Prejudice*, Elizabeth's powers of attraction simply cannot be denied. Similarly, in *Mansfield Park* Henry Crawford is originally described by the Bertram sisters as being "absolutely plain, black and plain" – though it is not long before he "was no longer allowed to be called so by any body", demonstrating the magical effect charm can have.

Nor is sex appeal gender specific: Jane Austen shows both men and women with the ability to appeal to the opposite sex. In the female category, step forward Elizabeth and Lydia Bennet from *Pride and Prejudice,* Marianne Dashwood from *Sense and Sensibility*, Mary Crawford in *Mansfield Park*, Emma Woodhouse from *Emma* and Lady Susan Vernon in *Lady Susan*. In the men's corner, we're looking at Willoughby in *Sense and Sensibility*, Wickham in *Pride and Prejudice*, Henry Crawford from *Mansfield Park*, Frank Churchill in *Emma* and Frederick Wentworth in *Persuasion*. Mr Darcy, although he has a great following in the real world, appeals to few within *Pride and Prejudice* itself.

Jane Austen also makes clear that sex appeal is often unconscious. Neither Elizabeth Bennet nor Marianne Dashwood make any attempt to attract men; and while Captain Wentworth

comes to Uppercross willing to be pleased and to find a wife, he does not intentionally attempt to captivate the local ladies.

Nonetheless, Jane Austen is not afraid of showing the darker side of sexual attraction. Henry Crawford intentionally flirts with both Julia and Maria Bertram, knowing exactly how far to go to keep each of them hoping that he might be seriously interested in her but without any intention of marriage: "He did not want them to die of love; but with sense and temper which ought to have made him judge and feel better, he allowed himself great latitude on such points." Later in *Mansfield Park*, Henry is also quite open about the fact that although he does not intend to marry her, he intends to make "a small hole in Fanny Price's heart"; and, although he originally claims that it is because of her lately improved looks, his remark that "I never was so long in company with a girl in my life – trying to entertain her – and succeed so ill… Her looks say, 'I will not like you, I am determined not to like you,' and I say, she shall" gives a more accurate picture of his true motive – injured pride. He is confident that he can do so, too; and Fanny's reaction to him shows that he is not entirely wrong to be that assured of success. Austen

IMAGE Dominic Cooper as Willoughby in *Sense and Sensibility* (2008)

writes that Fanny would no doubt have been persuaded into falling in love with him "had not her affection been engaged elsewhere". That Henry then falls for her and courts her seriously does not take away from his original intent. Of course, he then adds injury to insult by running off with the married Maria, even while still claiming himself as Fanny's suitor.

Intriguingly, there is a great similarity between Henry's reaction towards Fanny – first aiming to attract her to prove he can, but then falling for her – and his sister Mary's reaction to Edmund Bertram. Mary too undoubtedly deliberately uses her power of attraction early on in an attempt to captivate both Bertram brothers, just as Henry does with their two sisters. However, she actually does fall in love with Edmund Bertram and concentrates her attention on him despite him being the younger and therefore not going to come into the Bertram title. Edmund finally condemns her because she does not see how immoral and disgraceful her brother's actions have been; Mary is shown to be morally unaware. However, in many ways her lack of awareness is not so shameful as her attempts to use emotional blackmail to prevent Edmund becoming a cleric. While as a lady she cannot ask someone to marry her, her outspoken statement that "A clergyman is nothing" and her regular denigration of clerics and those who take holy orders makes her position quite clear – especially given that, unlike Henry with Fanny, she is in no doubt of Edmund's sentiments towards her.

In *Sense and Sensibility* and *Pride and Prejudice,* Willoughby and Wickham (respectively) are both shown to play upon their attractiveness to women for their own pleasure and gratification. Wickham is undoubtedly charming and universally liked in Meryton (Elizabeth's comment that out of Darcy and Wickham, "one has got all the goodness, and the other all the appearance of it" comes to mind here), yet has attempted to elope with a minor to gain her money, and takes Lydia to London with him with absolutely no intention of marrying her, thus ruining her reputation.

Willoughby's history is darker still, making Wickham's look almost acceptable and Henry Crawford's fairly minor. As well as marrying specifically for money during the course of the novel, before the action in *Sense and Sensibility* starts, he has seduced a girl and left her alone and with child – an act of which modern readers perhaps don't always realise the seriousness. In the 21st century we are accustomed to single mothers; but the moral crime was considered grave enough during the Regency period for Colonel Brandon, the girl's guardian, to challenge Willoughby – who, if not a friend, was certainly the friend of a friend – to a duel. The mother herself would have been shunned by polite society altogether.

Lust is a powerful force, and Jane Austen isn't afraid to show it. Even when characters are not intentionally using their sexual attractiveness to draw in others for devious ends, lust can be a damaging influence. No one could suggest that the Bennet parents have a happy marriage, for example; and it is made fairly clear that Mr Bennet's head was turned by a pretty face and attractive young woman. Near the very beginning of *Pride and Prejudice*, Mr Bennet comes close to making reference to it, telling his wife when she tells him that he needs to visit Mr Bingley that:

> *"You and the girls may go, or you may send them by themselves, which perhaps will be still better; for, as you are as handsome as any of them, Mr Bingley might like you the best of the party."*

> *"My dear, you flatter me. I certainly have had my share of beauty, but I do not pretend to be any thing extraordinary now. When a woman*

IMAGE Lust is a powerful force, and Jane Austen isn't afraid to show it in her writing – nor is Thomas Rowlandson in his drawings

Rowlandson 1815

Pub.d Feb.y 25 1815 by Tho.s Tegg N.o Cheapside.

NEIGHBOURLY REFRESHMENT.

has five grown up daughters, she ought to give over thinking of her own beauty."

"In such cases, a woman has not often much beauty to think of."

And talking of the Bennet family and their attractiveness, they make a good study in a range of different types of sexual attraction. One could argue for a sense of "high" and "low" sex appeal.

IMAGE *Fashionable Contrasts* by James Gillray showed a petite duchess's shoe next to the masculine feet of her lover

While Elizabeth Bennet attracts by her witty conversation and bright eyes, her youngest sister Lydia is quite happy to cater to the lower impulses, flirting unashamedly with any and every man in uniform she sees. Nevertheless, it would be unfair to say that Lydia does not have sex appeal: it is clear that she does by the fact that she, far more than Kitty Bennet, attracts men. Kitty would, it seems evident, like to have the same effect on men that Lydia does; it is equally evident that she does not. One can also only presume that Mrs Bennet had the same sort of appeal as Lydia

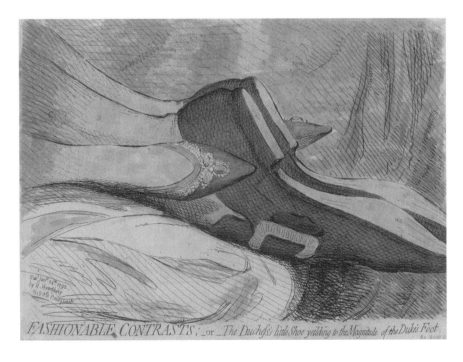

FASHIONABLE CONTRASTS; _or_ The Duchess's little Shoe yielding to the Magnitude of the Duke's Foot.

when she was young: she certainly understands and identifies with her youngest daughter more easily than with the other ones, and she could certainly (poor woman) never have had Elizabeth's wittiness!

Indeed, the Bennet family is fascinating to examine. Elizabeth has sex appeal without being conscious of it. Jane has a far gentler attraction, which is based more on being the archetypal "Madonna" type woman, and she would certainly never consider whether she was sexually appealing. Lydia has the sexiness of a vulgar flirt; and Kitty would like to have the same but cannot manage it. I suggest that Mary Bennet not only does not have sex appeal, but is painfully conscious of it. As someone without good looks or powers of attraction, it is hardly surprising that she focuses her attention on becoming "educated"; but it is unfortunate that she does not entirely succeed even here.

Given that Jane Austen clearly understands sex appeal so well, the way that she presents it is also very interesting. For in and of itself, there is nothing either good or bad about it. What it has is *power*: the power to draw other people in. In Jane Austen's world, and in Jane Austen's books, what matters is how you use those powers. Two hundred years after her death, is this perhaps not still a valid lesson?

PENELOPE FRIDAY

Penelop Friday is a writer with a special love for the Regency. As well as writing regularly for *Jane Austen's Regency World*, she has written two novels set in the period: *Petticoats and Promises* and *The Sisterhood*

• • • • •

CONCLUSION: THE JOY OF JANE

. . . . .

RICHARD JENKYNS look back at the first
two hundred years of Jane Austen's legacy

Perhaps Jane Austen needs more detractors. She has had them in the past: Charlotte Brontë was rather dismissive, and Mark Twain abusive. Kingsley Amis thought that *Mansfield Park* was the work of a mean-minded prig. Such criticisms, however misguided, can help to sharpen our sense of her and save us from stumbling into a bog of gooey adoration. But in recent years the dissenting voices seem to have fallen silent. Today she is probably the most read of classic English writers (and almost certainly the most re-read). She commands a huge middlebrow readership while keeping the admiration of the highbrows. She has even become a kind of British culture hero, and may indeed have replaced Dickens in the public imagination as *the* representative English novelist. How has she done it?

Because of the film and television adaptations, some will say. But that in itself is no explanation, because the

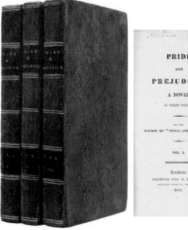

question is then why these adaptations have been so many and so popular. Some people have attributed her present appeal to nostalgia and a taste for sentimental romance: to the depiction of a safe and ordered world, or to fantasies of handsome men in tight britches and womanly bosoms throbbing beneath empire-line dresses. But if this has been a factor in her current success, it can only have been a small one. The idea that Jane Austen's world is safe and secure should not survive a reading of any of her books: anxieties over money, social insecurity and the fear of being left on the shelf are recurrent themes. *Pride and Prejudice* is, as its author herself said, "light and bright and sparkling", but no novel shows more clearly culture red in tooth and claw: when the family gets into trouble, they assume that their misfortunes will give pleasure to their neighbours. And if you hanker after Regency romance you will get more satisfaction out of Georgette Heyer, a writer of considerable accomplishment in her own way.

By contrast, Jane Austen is sometimes anti-glamorous: as Mrs Elton said about Emma's wedding: "Very little white satin, very few lace veils; a most pitiful business!" None of

IMAGE The first edition of *Pride and Prejudice* appeared in three volumes

her heroines marries badly, but only Elizabeth Bennet marries conspicuously well. Above all, her hard and ironic eye rebukes snobbery-fantasy. W. H. Auden imagined himself writing about her to Lord Byron:

> *You could not shock her more*
> *than she shocks me;*
> *Beside her Joyce seems innocent*
> *as grass.*
> *It makes me most uncomfortable*
> *to see*
> *An English spinster of the middle*
> *class*
> *Describe the amorous effects*
> *of 'brass',*
> *Reveal so frankly and with*
> *such sobriety*
> *The economic basis of society.*

That catches an important aspect of her: the sobriety of the surface and the frank glare shining through it. She is often a satirist and never a sentimentalist.

We do better to attribute her appeal today to two qualities which are in fact connected: her modernity and her realism or solidity. For most of history fiction has not been realistic (or even in prose). The "great tradition" of the literary realist novel, as we know it today, is surprisingly recent: essentially it originated in England in the 18th century and got its original impetus from two authors of genius, Samuel Richardson and Henry Fielding. These men are, on one view, the creators of the modern novel. But they are not completely modern: Richardson's epistolary method and Fielding's passages of epic burlesque set them at a certain distance from us. But a few externals aside, Jane Austen's books seem as contemporary as the latest novel about adultery in Hampstead. In this respect she is not only a modern novelist, but also the first modern novelist.

That notion gets confirmation from an uncomfortable truth about our own culture. Most people's reading does not go very deep into the past, and she is the earliest author in the English-speaking world who is read widely for pleasure. It is a pity that this is so, but the fact remains that it is so. Now there is no virtue to modernity in itself. Homer and Virgil are not modern, and that takes nothing away from them. There is a once-fashionable book by Jan Kott called *Shakespeare Our Contemporary*, but Shakespeare is not our contemporary and we should not want him to be so. Jane Austen's modernity is good not in itself but because it is inseparable from her realism: here are men and women with the loves, hopes and fears that we recognise in ourselves and in

> Jane Austen persuades us that her people inhabit a society that subsists beyond the printed page

those around us. She does not draw caricatures. "What about Mr Collins?" some will say, "or Miss Bates?" But the point is that such figures seem comic or preposterous to the other characters within the fiction, and people like that do exist in real life.

It is not an accident that her books have inspired more sequels than any other author's: readers feel that her characters are built in three dimensions, with such solidity that they continue to live and breathe beyond the page. No one wants to know how Fortinbras governed Denmark, or whether Pip found another woman to love, but many readers feel that they can intelligibly speculate about how the Wentworths or the Churchills might be doing twenty years on. And before we get too snooty about such games, we might note that Jane Austen herself was willing to play them with her family, telling them what was to happen to Mary Bennet and Mr Woodhouse in later years. One index of her solidity comes from those hints about off-stage characters whom we know only through what other people say about them. We never meet Miss Nash, but her pupil Harriet Smith talks about her, and through her artless chatter we get a vivid sense of the teacher's hopeless crush on Mr Elton; the prick of poignancy is distant and momentary, but it is very touching. Then there is Mrs Norris's rant over ten-year-old Dick Jackson, who tried vainly to stand up to her in a battle over the possession of two pieces of deal board; we shall never hear of him again, but briefly he is sturdily present in his attempt to stand up to an adult and a social superior. By such means Jane Austen persuades us that her people inhabit a society that subsists beyond the printed page. (One of her most telling portraits of a child, by the way, is of another ten-year-old, Charles Blake, in the fragmentary *Watsons*: first suffering a mortification and trying to stave off tears with "boyish bravery", and then, after

being rescued by the kindness of the heroine, making what he supposes to be interesting, grown-up conversation to her. Even in Jane Austen there are few more charming moments.)

She was five years younger than Beethoven (whose music, as far we can tell, she never heard). And all her novels concern a young woman who falls in love with a man and marries him. So it is easy to see her as an old-fashioned figure, a late representative of Augustan orderliness and decorum, someone who did conventional things with especial accomplishment. But she was actually an innovator, constantly experimenting. *Sense and Sensibility* is an experiment in writing a novel with two heroines. *Pride and Prejudice* is a perfect comedy of manners, and if that sounds traditional enough, try to think of an earlier novel – or indeed of any novel – that aims to be that. Or consider the book's first chapter, which is almost pure dialogue, without setting or explanation – an extraordinary experiment in writing a novel as though it were a play – and a play on a stage without any scenery, at that.

The later novels all explore unusual kinds of heroine. The heroine of *Persuasion* is faded and stuck on the shelf, her love story seemingly

IMAGE Joseph Karl Stieler's painting of Beethoven from 1820

over before the book has begun. Jane Austen notoriously thought of Emma as "a heroine that no one but myself will much like". This is also the first novel that gives a picture, indirectly, of a whole small society. It is also a study of immobility: Emma moves no more than half a dozen miles in the whole story. The most radical book of all is *Mansfield Park*. Again there is a strange heroine, seen first as a depressive child, and deliberately made to lack talents or accomplishments. And there are technical experiments in it. Most obviously, there is the use of the play *Lovers' Vows* as an ironic counterpoint to the personal relations of the people living at the Park – in the critical jargon, an exercise in intertextuality. More remarkable still is the scene at Sotherton where a locked door, a wilderness beyond and the threat of a torn dress are used symbolically to comment on Maria Bertram's sense of confinement and to look forward to her future adultery. Astonishingly, this is where symbolism begins.

Comedy was her chosen mode, and she knew her limits. She was perfectly sincere when she told the Prince Regent's librarian that she was incapable of taking a heroic theme and that she was among the most ignorant of authors, even though she made the point in humorous language. But like Shakespeare she could stretch the bounds of comedy pretty wide. In the creation of comic characters she rivals Dickens, and in giving such characters roundedness and complexity she far outclasses him. She was also a mistress of that most difficult art of making characters who are funny not because we laugh at them but because we laugh with them, as she showed in the creation of Elizabeth Bennet and her father. Cleverer still, she gives the two of them different styles of wit: his humour is made out of verbal incongruities, hers from amusing ideas. But in all her novels (even in *Northanger Abbey*, though least so there) she found a means of combining comedy with ethical weight, with the serious study of how men and women live and make their choices. And at times she hardly seems to be writing comedy at all. Many readers have felt that *Persuasion* has an autumnal quality to it (although this feeling may be influenced by the knowledge that it was to be her last work). We can be fairly sure from the start that the ending will be happy, not only because of the broad comedy of the opening page but because otherwise Anne Elliot's story has no direction in which to develop, but the book's tone has a sobriety that is unique to it. *Mansfield Park* is hardly a comedy at all: the tone is sometimes bitter and the action seems to come to a close with almost everyone ruined or wrecked.

The "happy ending", in which Fanny gets her man after all, is presented, very briefly, as a kind of postscript.

Jane Austen's family was unusually healthy. None of her brothers or sisters died in infancy and all of them except herself lived to a reasonably ripe age. She might well have ended her career as a Victorian novelist. What would those unwritten books have been like? As with Mozart's works of the 1820s and Schubert's of the 1850s, we shall never know. But in *Sanditon*, the fragment on which she was working before she became too ill to write, we see her still trying new things: an urban setting, property development as a theme, the lubricious fantasies of a young aristocrat (the first and last time that she presents the inner thoughts of a male). Perhaps she would have moved in radically new directions, perhaps not. As it is, we are left with a writer whose life was circumscribed in duration as well as in experience. Modern though she is, in important senses, she was of course a woman of her time – but in a distinctive way, for she is both an 18th-century stoic and a 19th-century romantic, and a moralist whose morals are wrapped in irony. That complexity enriches her work. We re-read Jane Austen to laugh once more at famous scenes and be happy again in the heroines' ultimate happiness, but in re-reading we may also come to feel

more strongly how moving she can be. There are moments of keen poignancy and penetration: when Wentworth takes the child off Anne Elliot's back; when Mr Bennet briefly drops the mask and obliquely confesses to Elizabeth the emptiness of his marriage; when Mary comes to the east room to cajole Fanny into marrying Henry and is jolted from her course by her memories of Edmund in that place. Of course we delight in the joy of Jane Austen's glittering surface, but there is joy to be found in exploring the depth of her too.

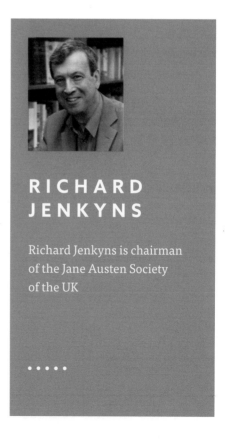

RICHARD JENKYNS

Richard Jenkyns is chairman of the Jane Austen Society of the UK

• • • • •

IMAGES

06 Sue Pomeroy

07 Express Newspapers

08 Newsshopper; Library of Congress

11 n/k

12 British Library

16 National Archive

17 Ellen Hill

18 John Buckler

19 Angelo Hornak/Alamy

23 JAHM x2

24 Buena Vista International

26 BBC

27 BBC

33 NLA

34 Edward Steichen (1903)

35 Jane Austen Memorial Trust

36 NPG

37 DNB (c1930)

38 OUP

40 NPG

43 Josephine Sittenfeld

44 Lionsgate

45 JAC

46 NLS/Murray Archive

48 Barker Evans

49 Constance Hill

53 Sir Henry Raeburn/NGS

54 Benjamin Robert Haydon/NPG

55 istock

56 George Charles Beresford

58 AP

61 n/k

63 BBC

64 King's College, Cambridge

66 n/k

69 Alan Weller

71 JAHM

72 Owen Benson/JAC

74 n/k

76 Patrick Stokes

79 CE Brock

80 Bath in Time

82 The Times

84 Tim Bullamore

85 Tim Bullamore

89 NPG

90 NPG

91 Francis Austen

92 Richard Bentley (1871)

93 Bank of England

94 n/k

95 HM Brock

97 Melissa Dring/JAC; artist unknown

99 Melissa Dring/JAC

100 Rice family

103 Borders Ancestry

104 James Gillray/Trustees of the British Museum

105 William Holland/Trustees of the British Museum

106 Gentleman's Magazine

110 World History Archive/Alamy

113 William Henry Mote (1855)

115 BBC

116 BBC

119 Thomas Rowlandson/Royal Collection

120 James Gillray/Hannah Humphrey

122 T Egerton

125 Beethoven Haus, Bonn